The Encyclopedia of Antique Postcards

"Keep Smiling, never mind the Bills"

My Favorite Postcard

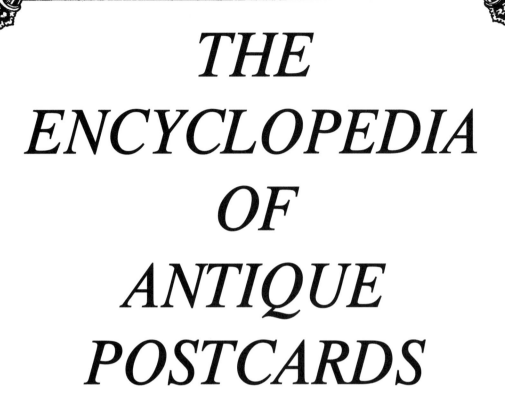

THE ENCYCLOPEDIA OF ANTIQUE POSTCARDS

by Susan Brown Nicholson

Fully Illustrated with Price Guide

WALLACE-HOMESTEAD BOOK COMPANY
Radnor, Pennsylvania

Dedicated to William Arthur Brown (July 8, 1917 - May 13, 1992)

Susan Brown Nicholson, a graduate of Iowa State University, has been a contributing editor to many publications on antiques, including *Collector's Showcase*, *Spinning Wheel*, *Doll Reader*, *Antique Toy World*, *Hobbies* and *The Teddy Bear and Friends*.

Nicholson, a recognized authority on paper ephemera, writes monthly columns on antique postcards and their values for *Barr's Postcard News* and *The Postcard Collector*. She provides the prices for several sections of each edition of *Warman's Americana and Collectibles* guide and has lectured to the National Association of Dealers of Antiques, on rare and expensive postcards.

Nicholson has written: *Teddy Bears on Paper*, *Mickey Mouse Memorabilia* and *The Antique Postcards of Rose O'Neill*. She has collected antique paper memorabilia for 25 years.

Copyright ©1994 by Susan Brown Nicholson

All Rights Reserved

Published in Radnor, Pennsylvania 19089, by Wallace-Homestead,
a division of Chilton Book Company

Manufactured in the United States of America

Library of Congress Cataloging-in-Publication Data
Nicholson, Susan Brown.
    Encyclopedia of antique postcards/Susan Brown Nicholson.
      p. cm.
    Includes index.
    ISBN 0-87069-730-7
    1. Postcards. I. Title.
NC1872.N53   1994
741.6'83'03—dc20   94-14084
                                                  CIP

1 2 3 4 5 6 7 8 9 0   3 2 1 0 9 8 7 6 5 4

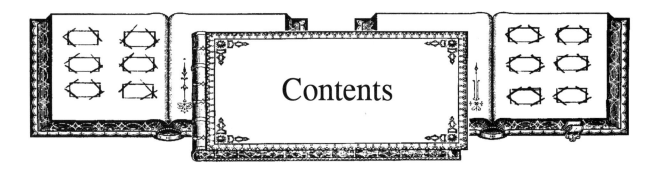

Contents

CONTENTS

CONTENTS

Acknowledgements

No one writes a book alone, and this type of book in particular. Without the shared knowledge of other collectors, dealers and many authors in the bibliography, this work would not be possible. Compiling this book can best be described with Michel Eyquem de Montaigne's words, a French writer from the sixteenth century, "I gather the flowers by the wayside, by the brooks and in the meadows, and only the string with which I bind them together is my own."

My foremost thanks go to James H. Nicholson, my husband, who did the photography, layout, and editing. Without his persistence and attention to detail, this book would never have been completed.

I thank everyone for their contributions to this volume.

Chuck and Jan Banneck
David Bonomo
Andreas Brown
George and Ellen Budd
V. Lee and Shirley Cox
Ron de Bijl
Ben Duncan
John and Lynn Farr
George Gibbs
Jocelyn Howells
Fred Kahn
Jack and Michael Leach
Bill and Mary Martin

George Miller
John and Sandy Millns
Dan Miranda
Walter Mitchell
John and Nancy Mordock
Jim Morrison
Rita Nadler
Hal Ottaway
Lois Pietz
Dorothy Ryan
DeDe and Daisy Schaeffer
Gene Semel
Jonah and Marty Shapiro

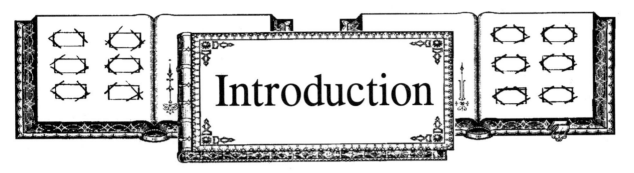

Introduction

Mailing

Collecting

During the middle 1800s, both lithography and photography were used for souvenir pictures of tourist attractions and special events in the major cities of the world. These were produced in full color, sepia, and even blue tones.

These early souvenirs were produced in 2½ by 4 inch carte de visite size, then cabinet size and stereoscope sets. There was an abundance of this material made in America and Europe preceding the postcard. There were illustrated letter sheets, valentines, and New Years and Christmas greeting cards used during the 1840s and 1850s. During the Civil War (1861-1865) patriotic letterheads and envelopes were extensively used. This beginning of decorative items to be mailed led to the development of the picture postcard.

John P. Charlton, Philadelphia, obtained a copyright on a private postal card in 1861. When he applied for a patent, it was refused. He sold his copyright to H.L. Lipman of Philadelphia, who produced and sold the *Lipman's Postal Card*. It was a non-pictorial message card with a stamp box and address line on one side and a blank message space on the other. These cards were used until 1873 when the United States issued the government postal. Advertisers used Lipman cards to print messages and illustrations. He was considered the father of the modern mailing cards.

A similar card was used in Belgium in 1864. In 1865, Dr. Heinrich von Stephan, from Germany, proposed the postal card while attending the Austro-German Postal Conference. The idea was rejected. Heinrich von Stephan's complete speech can be found in Frank Staff's book, *The Picture Postcard and its Origin*.

A few years later, Dr. Emanuel Hermann of Vienna,

INTRODUCTION

an economics professor, proposed the postcard again, this time, greatly impressing the Austrian Post Office. On October 1, 1869, the world's first government postal card was born. Austria sold these postal cards, with imprinted stamps, that were called *Correspondenz Karte.*

Germany disputed Doctor Hermann's claim, as the inventor of the postcard, but there is no doubt that Austria produced the first government postal. During the first three months after being issued, nearly 3 million cards were sold.

Facing and Assorting

This great success caused other countries to join Austria in producing postcards. North Germany followed in July, 1870, South Germany followed next and the United Kingdom in October, 1870.

The idea spread across Europe with Belgium and Holland introducing their postcards on January 1, 1871. Three months later cards were on sale in Denmark, Norway and Sweden. Canada introduced a card in 1871, Russia in 1872 and France

Mode of Transportation to Office

in 1873. The United States rejected the idea in 1870 but embraced it, June 8, 1872, with 60 million cards sold in the last six months of 1873.

It wasn't until later that the early government postal cards were allowed to be sent internationally. An agreement reached at the first Postal Congress made this possible. This first International Postal Treaty took effect July 1, 1875.

Please remember these were all government postals.

While the purchaser of these cards printed and even illustrated the messages, they were not commercially produced picture postcards. Some postal cards were printed with patriotic and humorous designs to be sold to the troops of France and Prussia. Burdick's book, *Pioneer Postcards*, fully discusses and illustrates these government postal cards.

In the United States, pictorial advertisements, and Christmas and New Year's greetings were printed on government postals. During this period, these cards were called pioneers. The pioneers carry instructions like, *Write the address only on this side-the message on the other.* Later, *Nothing but the address can be placed on this side,* and *This side for the address only* or similar words.

In 1898, Congress provided privately published postcards the same standards and rates as government

2

Distributing to Carriers

postals. These postcards were inscribed, *Private Mailing Card—Authorized by the Act of Congress, May 19, 1898.*

Eventually the regulations eased and the words *Post Card* could be used to distinguish the private cards from government *Postal Cards*. Further concessions came in 1902 in England, 1904 in France, 1905 in Germany and 1907 in the United States when a postcard back was divided. This allowed one half for the message, the other for the address. Before this, many postcards were designed with message space on the front of the card. These regulations allowed the entire front of the card to be used for design.

This information serves as a historical background of the picture postcard, but a definition is necessary for the term postcard. It has always been possible to mail any piece of paper by affixing the proper postage. There were early photographs, album trade cards and greeting cards mailed, but this does not give them postcard status. To quote Burdick, an early researcher of the picture post card, "The criterion is not that a card has been, or could be, sent through the mail but that the card was made with the intention that it could be used by itself as a mailed message or souvenir."

Because of confusion about postal rates, the widespread use of the cards was not until the 1890s. Some postcards illegally made it through the system at one cent each; while others, which legally should have been mailed for one cent, were detained for a two cent rate.

As important as the mail regulations were, it was the establishment of the Rural Free

RURAL FREE DELIVERY

Delivery system in 1898, that made the postcard a universal tool. Before this act, only homes in towns of ten thousand or more had free delivery. All others had to travel great distances to post letters and rarely had an easy way to receive mail. By 1906, Rural Free Delivery was well established and sending postcards became a way of life.

The World Columbian Exposition of 1893 issued several sets of picture postcards, featuring the Fair's attractions, printed on government postal cards. However, it was the picture postcards issued after 1898, without imprinted postage, which started the card collecting craze in the United States.

From 1898 to 1918 a phenomenon called the *Golden Age of Postcards* emerged. Both adults and children were obsessed with buying, sending and collecting postcards. Billions were mailed throughout the world. There were even postcard collecting clubs where individuals met to exchange cards and share their albums.

Postcard publishers worked day and night to meet the demand for cards. Postcards were sold in drugstores, news stands, dime stores, souvenir shops and even specialty shops that sold only postcards. Postcards of tourist attractions in major cities were sold by the thousands on every street corner. This explains why so many postcards of this type still exist.

Publishers wanting to benefit financially from the postcard collecting craze, used an ingenious idea. They produced postcards in sets, to persuade the public to buy several postcards rather than just one.

The sets may have started with a simple days of the week or months of the year grouping. It blossomed into artists illustrating groups of four, six, twelve, or twenty-four cards all with a common theme, such as flower children. Other sets contain postcards that have very little relationship to one another, other than a common series number.

The most interesting sets are those that tell a complete story from start to finish. While an individual card might be appealing, it may not be truly understood until the complete set is assembled.

For example, one Easter

card of a hen vigorously shaking her umbrella in the air, is only part of the story. The second card, showing a rooster dropping and breaking eggs, explains the anger of the hen.

Sets provided the publisher and retailer with bonus sales. Customers may have come looking for one set, but purchased more cards from the store's stock. Sets were designed for nearly every topic: social and historic events, col-

lege girls, famous people, presidents, artists, horoscopes, ad promotions, comic characters, and holidays.

During the postcard craze, there were 45 states. Several sets pertain to the capitols of these states or state girls. Religious sets featured the Ten Commandments and the Lord's Prayer. Highly collected artist's sets were the Sunbonnet babies, the teddy bear, and Rose O'Neill's Kewpies. Every holiday was celebrated with postcards, even Labor Day and Groundhog Day.

The postcard became highly successful as an inexpensive way to send short messages. Mail was collected and delivered as often as three times a day. The phrase, "Drop me a line" was prevalent until telephone service replaced it with, "Call me."

Raphael Tuck was a well known English firm with high

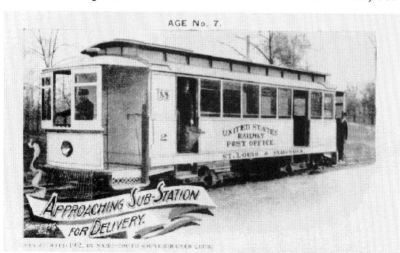

Approaching Sub-Station For Delivery

standards for production of greeting cards when they decided to enter postcard publishing. Their marketing skills sur-

passed all others. In 1900 they organized a competition that was advertised on the back of postcard packets. The packet stated, "With a view of fostering the love of Art, and encouraging the collecting of artistic post cards, Prizes to the amount

of 1000 pounds will be awarded to the Collectors of the largest number of TUCK'S POST CARDS that have passed through the post no matter to whom addressed..." These contests continued with the prize

Carriers Routing Mail

money increasing through time.

This created a fever of collecting that has never returned. From 1907, it is reported "...

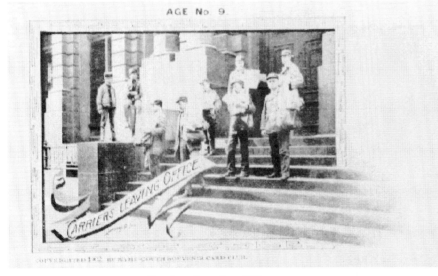

Carriers Leaving Office

the Picture Postcard is the best guide to the spirit of the Edwardian era. For the Picture

Postcard is a candid revelation of our pursuits and pastimes, our customs and costumes, our morals and manners."

James Douglas, a London journalist and author, reported the real benefits of the post-card. Before the postcard, men were required to write lengthy letters to their friends. Douglas reporting the postcards virtues, stated, "It has secretly delivered us from the toil of letter writing... Our forefathers actually sat down and wasted hours over those long epistles... It is sad to think of the books that dead authors might have written if they had saved the hours which they squandered upon private correspondence... Formerly, when a man went abroad he was forced to tear himself from the scenery in order to write laborious descriptions of it to his friends at home. Now he merely buys a picture

INTRODUCTION

postcard at each station... nobody need fear that there is any spot on the earth which is not depicted on this wonderful oblong. The photographer has photographed everything between the poles. He has snapshotted the earth. No mountain and no wave has evaded his omnipresent lens. The click of his shutter has been heard on every Alp and in every desert. He has hunted down every landscape and seascape on the globe. Every bird and every beast has been captured by the camera. It is impossible to gaze upon a ruin without finding a picture postcard of it at your elbow. Every pimple on the earth's skin has been photographed, and wherever the human eye roves or roams it detects the self conscious air of the reproduced... The Picture Postcard carries rudeness to the fullest extremity, there is no room for anything polite. Now and then one can write on a blue sky or a white road, but, as a rule, there is no space for more than a gasp..."

A revival of the hobby has sparked more interest in postcards in the last ten years than the previous decades. The news media has become interested in the high prices some cards have obtained and in the notable people who have collections.

One appealing aspect of collecting postcards is that there is so much unknown and unrecorded that keeps most collector's interests peaked. The number of books in the bibliography give example to the collector's desire for information. It is even more exciting to find a postcard that has been previously unrecorded. This is where knowledge is power. Without the information already in print it is impossible to know what is common or rare without investing years collecting and making mistakes.

This book contains many unusual postcards to hold the interest of the advanced collector, but it is written to educate the novice. When the work of a common artist is illustrated, such as Ellen Clapsaddle, uncommon examples are used. Not much space is used illustrating artists for which entire books have been written. These artists include Brundage, Clapsaddle, Fisher, Boileau and O'Neill. If you wish more information on these artists, consult the Bibliography and Sources sections.

The price guide is just that, a *guide*, not prices written in stone. It will help you sort out which cards are $2 each and which are $200. It will not tell you this card always sells for $2.35. A variety of material is priced, even cards that are not illustrated. Several professional dealers were consulted on the pricing to provide a broader perspective. Prices on rare postcards jump quickly and certain categories become hot, causing some areas of any price guide to become obsolete.

In the last ten years, postcard prices have soared, out performing most investments. Like art, investing in postcards is speculative as they are not easily liquidated. Investment in postcards should be done with much study and the advice of professional dealers.

Postcard collecting is fun. It doesn't take up much room and unlike many other collectibles, you can set comfortable financial restraints. Some collectors set allowances of $20 per show, others $2000. Both have fun. §

Delivery By Carrier

> *In 1902, the Name-Couth Souvenir Card Club published, for the World's Fair City of St. Louis, a ten card set featuring the process of the postal service (illustrated here with titles).*

Beginners

If you are a novice collector and are trying to evaluate an accumulation of postcards, READ THIS FIRST.

If your postcards are in an album with deteriorating pages, that look like black or green construction paper, carefully remove each card. Be sure not to damage the corners. These old albums have protected the cards from damage and light for 60 to a 100 years. But, they contain acid that will eventually cause the cards to fox, which are small brown spots. Most old empty postcard albums have very little monetary value, unless they have unusually decorated covers or high quality interior pages.

Now, you are ready to evaluate your card collection. Divide the cards into two groups; views of places and topics, such as holidays.

VIEWS

The view cards can be sorted by state or country. While this book does not contain illustrated information

"A Card to the Kiddies"

about view cards, there are multiple criteria by which to judge your cards. Views of large

major cities are generally common. The exceptions are real photo cards that depict a small part of these cities. For example, while New York City postcards are easy to find, real photo postcards of Greenwich Village are not common.

Most small town postcard views are more valuable than those of large cities. Examine your small town views that look like actual photographs, but have a post card logo on the back. These are called *real photo* views and are the most prized. Itinerant photographers who traveled from town to town and local photographers generally produced them in small quantities.

The view cards of the main street and the train depot are highly collectible. Main street views are more interesting if they contain people, horse drawn vehicles or automobiles.

A circus on the main street adds even more value. The views of depots increase in value if the train is in the station.

Views of the exteriors of schools, churches, and store

This is for you

fronts are collected and easier to find. Views of parks are common and seldom of much value. Interior views of barber shops, schools, grocery stores, and blacksmith shops are very collectible. Postcards featuring horse drawn Rural Free Delivery, popcorn, or Watkins wagons are the most valuable type of view card. These real photo postcard views need to be identified by the city and state, or city and country, of origin.

States that were sparsely populated at the turn of the century, had few cards printed of their small towns. These bring the highest prices. The most expensive view cards are of small towns in states like, Nevada, Oklahoma, and Califor-

nia. Like all collectibles, it takes several interested collectors to establish a market. Some state postcards are not collected at all due to the lack of interested persons from or in that state. This gap of unsalable state material is narrowing every day.

It is important to remember that real photo postcards are the most collected, while the commercially printed view cards are of less value. The same criteria apply in Europe. Small town life is prized, while metropolitan Paris and castles or cathedrals of England are less desirable.

Use common sense to evaluate view cards. If lots and lots of people visited the place illustrated on the card, it is probably common. This brings us to World War I and II. While no disrespect is intended, in terms of postcards, these wars were the biggest tourist attractions. Millions of cards were sold to thousands and thousands of soldiers on both sides. Most of these cards were sent or brought back home. Postcards of bombs exploding, bombed buildings, military leaders and soldiers are all easy to find. This does not mean they are not collected; just that they are more reasonably priced.

To sell view cards, the best place is in the town, state, or country of origin. If you have a large collection of Indiana and you live in West Virginia, local dealers will not be as interested as a dealer in Indiana. Ads in

trade papers or contacts with dealers in Indiana are important. Consult the Sources section of this book for addresses of trade papers.

Many turn of the century postcards were published abroad. European and English postcard companies kept offices and agents in the United States. Anyone could contact one of these agents and have cards printed from their original artwork for a very nominal fee. It is, therefore, impossible to identify every postcard publisher since some may have done only one design. One reference attempting to record all publishers, lists over 1500 different companies.

To my Sweetheart

The largest publishers of American scenic cards were Hammon of Chicago and Minneapolis, Kropp of Milwaukee, Detroit Publishing Company of Detroit, Illustrated Postal Card Company of New York,

INTRODUCTION

Mitchell of San Francisco, The Souvenir Postcard Company of New York, Curt Teich and Company of Chicago, and Leighton Company of Portland, Maine. Leighton later merged with Valentine & Sons Publishing Company of New York and London.

TOPICS

To evaluate non-view postcards, first sort them by topics such as holidays, advertising, political, or publisher. While it may seem hard to sort by publisher, it really isn't that difficult. During the Golden Age (1898-1918), each post card company had a special style or logo for the words *Post Card* on the back. Turn the cards over and sort them according to what the words *Post Card* look like. Then examine the fronts and notice how similar the cards are in style, design and quality.

Major publishing houses such as Tuck, Winsch, Whitney, Paul Finkenrath, and Detroit are highly collected. Yet, just because a card says *TUCK* doesn't mean it is valuable. Many Tuck cards sell for ten cents, and few sell for over $30. The difference is in rarity, quality of art work and condition. While there are many rare and expensive postcards, few of these are because they are Tuck,

Winsch, PFB or Detroit.

Again, when looking at the non-view postcards use common sense. Which do you think would be harder to find, a Christmas card or a Ground Hog Day card? Few publishers made Ground Hog Day cards, while most publishers made Christmas cards. Think about the holidays. We still send cards for Christmas, Easter, Thanksgiving, and Valentine's Day.

These are all easy to find in vintage postcards. The most common greeting card is the birthday card. Again, common sense tells us, we probably send more birthday cards in a year than Halloween cards.

This does not mean all birthday postcards are worthless.

Many birthday postcards do sell in the ten cent boxes, but if the card is signed by an artist like Clapsaddle, Brundage, or O'Neill, it may be valuable. These artist signed cards are highly collected. The signatures are often hidden in or near the design elements of the postcards.

ARTIST SIGNED

For the beginner, we must clearly state we are *not* referring to postcards autographed by the postcard artist, while a few of these do exist. We are totally concerned with cards where the original art work was signed and this signature was carried over into the printing process. Occasionally, the artwork was signed only to have the entire picture cropped and the signature completely or partially lost in the resulting printed postcard. If an artist has a particularly easy style to recognize, the work does not need to be signed to be collectable.

Just because an artist did not sign or only signed by initials or monograms that have not been identified, does not mean that the postcard is not collectible. While many people collect H.B.G. (Griggs), to date no one has even found evidence whether this artist is a man or a woman. Many very capable postcard artists remain anonymous.

INTRODUCTION

Artists who were very good did much of this unsigned work, but considered themselves *fine* artists not commercial artists. They may have taken a postcard commission to pay the rent. Seeing it only as a job, not as art, they may not have wanted to sign the work.

Yet, art and illustration was considered an honorable profession for women during the Golden Age of postcards and many women found it a rewarding job. This was when few professions were considered suitable for women. Teaching, child care, nursing, and the arts were among the most acceptable occupations. While most of these had very little monetary reward, art illustration would support women artists in some degree of comfort. Others, who were wise enough to control the copyright of their characters, such as Rose O'Neill and her Kewpie, could amass fortunes.

Most artists worked for only one or two publishers. Once you sort your cards by publisher or similar styles, signed cards can be found. The artists listed in this book are among the most collected. The more information known about an artist; the more it is collected. Also, the more cards a person produced; the more they are collected. Entire books have been written about

Ellen Clapsaddle and Frances Brundage (see Sources).

HOLIDAYS

To evaluate the holiday postcards start with New Year's Day. The most collected are those by the publisher John Winsch and Raphael Tuck or artist signed cards by O'Neill and Griggs, others are common. Any holiday card that is a Hold to Light has value.

Collectible Valentine's Day cards are those published by Tuck, Winsch and PFB, artist signed cards, and cards that are just graphically attractive.

Saint Patrick's Day is not

This is from us

highly collected. Most cards are green with motifs of shamrocks, Blarney Stones, pipes and pa-

rades and appeal to a small collector base.

Easter cards are common. The most desirable images feature dressed animals.

Fourth of July cards seem to gain popularity at times when patriotism is high, as during the bicentennial. These cards are extremely colorful and fun, but under collected.

Halloween is a very collected holiday postcard. The images range from $2 to $300. The most valuable are the cards designed by Samuel L. Schmucker for John Winsch Publishing. No one has recorded a vintage Hold to Light Halloween postcard. The Clapsaddle Halloween mechanicals are highly collected, especially the postcard featuring the Black child.

Thanksgiving is not very collected, perhaps because the cards generally lack interesting design and have muted colors. Samuel Schmucker, for Winsch Publishing, did the best work for this holiday, including some projection cards that feature small die cut pieces that project out from the cards. There are some interesting Hold to Lights and mechanicals. The cards featuring Uncle Sam or Lady Liberty with a turkey are more desirable. Generally, few cards of this holiday sell for more than $20 each.

INTRODUCTION

Christmas has the largest selection of cards and the most collectors. While the supply is high, so is the demand. The most collected is Santa Claus. They are divided into Santas in red suits and Santas in other than red suits. The latter bring higher prices. The most valuable Santas are black faced, installment and Hold to Light Santas. The rarest Santa cards are the Hold to Light Santas dressed as Uncle Sam.

Postcards for Ground Hog Day and Labor Day are highly desirable and scarce.

OTHER TOPICS

Other valuable non-view cards feature advertising, politics, prohibition, suffrage, and expositions. These cards are collected because they portray the social and political history of the times. At the turn of the century, news sources did not include radio, television, or even a daily newspaper. Postcards served as a way to tell the story and reach the public with a message for very little cost. Most cards sold for a penny and could be mailed for a penny. Since these cards were the junk mail of the time, many were thrown away while the birthday card sent to your mother was saved.

Again, put on that common sense cap and think about how many were made, whether they were likely to be thrown away, or whether they were likely to be saved as souvenirs. Advertising postcards from expositions and fairs are more common than those advertising small local companies.

Now, having gone through this sorting and touching process, you will have a better understanding of what you have. There are exceptions to every rule. Some very rare cards are beautiful and you can't imagine anyone throwing them away, but so are some very common cards. Some rare cards are so dull and unimaginative, you can't understand anyone saving them, but so are some common cards.

CONDITION

The prices in this book are for mint to near mint cards. This means they look like they were printed today. There are no exceptions.

It is always hard for a novice to realize that so many cards survived in this excellent to mint condition. A card with a corner crease may be worth ten cents, while the identical card in mint condition is worth five dollars. Collectors are very condition conscious.

Poor condition is never tolerated on common cards. Only in recent years has poor condition become acceptable on scarce cards. Some minor flaws are tolerated on rare material, but the price is expected to be adjusted accordingly. In other words, a rare card in poor condition may be salable if the price is right. A common card in poor condition should only be kept if it has sentimental value.

What detracts from the condition? Any defect affecting the image detracts from the price of the card. Things such

as: cancel marks on the picture side, hand writing on the front, creases, tears, foxing, and soil, detract from the value. The more that is wrong with the card; the more its value drops. Written on or postally used cards are not less valuable, if it does not affect the image side. Many beginning collectors like canceled cards because it seems to offer assurances of age, which may or may not be true. Some collectors will pay more for a postcard that has an interesting message about the illustration or the social times.

Condition is not everything. Since more and more collectors have entered the hobby, condition has become a compromise between wanting the card and waiting to find it in better shape. Most collectors take the card, at a reduced price, and watch to upgrade their collection. Rare cards are always accepted with defects, but not at a premium price.

You may purchase cards you feel are rare, with corners missing, blurred ink on the front and a chewed up, spit out, ironed flat look, just to have an example, but never at a premium price. Truely rare cards usually appear only about every ten years.

Generally, cards in that condition are garbage and dealers regularly throw them away. However, they can be given to children to start a collection, or donated to libraries or schools for display.

SELLING YOUR CARDS

To a novice collector, it is very hard to evaluate your cards without help. This book is a start, but more information can be gained by sitting with a professional dealer and discussing what you have. This is best done near the end of a postcard show, as the opening hours are very hectic and prime money making time for the dealers. Or, cards can be sent to dealers for appraisals or offers.

If you plan to sell your postcards to a dealer don't expect to get full retail price. The only way to get the full price is to pay $100-500 for a single table at a show, drive to that show, pay for out-of-town lodging, food, and sit for an entire weekend with the chance a collector will come by that wants the postcards. Don't begrudge the dealer a reasonable profit for their hard work and expenses.

You can advertise the cards in trade papers or do mail auctions, but again that requires lots of work. If you want to sell all the postcards, not just the rare ones, it will take a willing dealer.

You can get several opinions, but, if a dealer is willing to give you the time to appraise your collection carefully and makes a fair offer, don't be greedy. Another dealer may say, "I'll top any offer by five dollars." These dealers have not done the appraisal work and are taking advantage of their dealer colleagues.

If you do not want to sell the cards, but want an appraisal, tell the dealer up front. If the appraisal is retail and seems high to you and you decide to sell, don't expect to get that price. Tell the dealer, "I had no idea they had that much value. What could you pay me and still make a profit?"

If the collection has sentimental value but the monetary value is in only a few cards, they could be sold. Unless they have very special meaning to your family, you can have your cake and eat it too. By selling two or three postcards, you can save the remainder of the collection for your family history.

FAMILY HISTORY

If you have a family album and intend to keep it, do everything to document the photographic cards of family members. These cards have little or no monetary value unless they feature an unusual doll, toy or peddle car in the picture.

Pencil, remember pencil, lightly as much information as you can gather. This includes the full name, birth and death date, where buried, city of birth, relationship to other family names, and date when photo was taken. These are the most important facts.

The cards can be shown to elderly relatives and the stories they tell recorded on tape. Ask questions like, "What was your sister like?" and "Where did you go to school?" Remember to listen and learn. Many cards are inscribed "taken five years ago," "Aunt Sadie," or "Bessie's daughter." Most of these notations have no meaning one generation later when they are often sold for a quarter. They should be a part of a family history. This is good advice for all family photographs, even the ones taken this week. §

The six cards illustrated are from series number 2129 published by B. B. London and printed in Saxony.

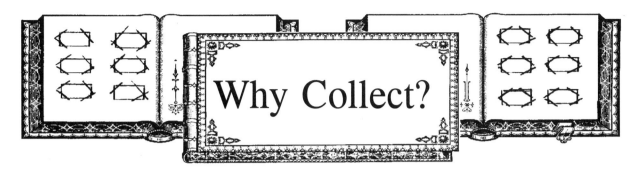

Why Collect?

People may collect postcards because of the nostalgia for their youth or even the longing for a time never experienced. It is fun to see postcards of the main street of the town where you or your parents were raised. When looking at the real photo postcards, we can see how the turn of the century family dressed, lived, worked, traveled and died. Yes, even departed family members were depicted on photographic postcards.

Antique postcards reflect the past; modern postcards contemporary times. Cards tell us of the social climate of whatever era we examine, whether it is the suffrage movement of the early 1900s or the Equal Rights Amendment of the 1980s. They tell us about a disappearing past, like houses decorated from gutter to ground for Flag Day, steam train travel, and farming with horse drawn plows.

Collecting scenic postcards saves a piece of what existed before the flood, fire or wrecking ball took its toll. Even these disasters are recorded on postcards. They remind us of where we went to school, church or movies. Many of these places are gone or changed beyond recognition. Postcards hold memories.

Postcard collecting is fun because it's less expensive than many other collecting interests, takes very little space to enjoy, and covers every possible subject. In fact, a postcard collector, via mail auctions, can collect without even leaving their home.

Because of the large diversity of postcard material available for sale today, a collector can enjoy the hobby for as little as 25-50 cents per card. In this price range, collectors buy cards of yellow roses, Chicago views, birthday greetings, cats illustrated by unknown artists, modern social history, windmills, castles, parks, Easter crosses, and much more.

Commercial companies produced picture postcards as collector's items from the beginning. The Golden Age of postcards, 1898-1918, saw every parlor with card albums on the table. Many were designed

"HOBBIES"

Picture Postcard Collecting.

Dear I'm busy! Hungry--so sorry! Little Mary has been busy all day--but never mind darling, you can wait.

in sets to satisfy this Victorian collecting craze.

During this time millions of cards were published, and a great many of these were mailed. The New York City post office, at the turn of the century, would handle as many as 30,000 per day. In 1909, Americans purchased over one billion postcards, about twice what today's industry sells per year. In 1904, Germany sent over 1 billion postcards, France 600 million, Japan 453 million, Austria 250 million, Belgium 55 million and even Switzerland 43 million.

The cards, that are hardest to find today, relate to special interests of the Golden Age. Many advertising cards were treated as junk mail and discarded. Political campaign cards were tossed out with regularity. Cards relating to the pro-suffrage movement are rarely found mailed, which leads you to believe those cards were hand exchanged or saved only by those active in the cause. Yet, cards such as simple birthday greetings were printed in abundance at the turn-of-century. How do we know? Because millions of these cards have survived and can easily be purchased for less than a dollar.

Postcards were often sold for a penny and could be mailed for one or two cents during most of the Golden Age. This made them particularly attractive for correspondence and collectors.

The history of the scientific world and modernization of the domestic world are recorded on postcards. That era saw transportation change from the horse and buggy to automobiles and airplanes. The home became modernized with tele-

DEAREST, YOURS' ARE THE ONLY POSTCARDS I KEEP

phones, electric lights, radios, and indoor plumbing. All of which is recorded on postcards. Many of these newfangled devices, like the electric light, first appeared on postcards illustrated by comic artists. Later, outhouses were made fun of on

postcards after plumbing became common place.

The picture postcard brought art to the common man. Many postcards published were not original art, but reproductions of contemporary and old masters. The postcards of artists like Alphonse Mucha were generally reprints of larger works. The publishers Stengel, of Dresden, Germany, and Sbjorb, of Florence, Italy, produced high quality reproductions of museum artwork. These cards were printed on the best quality paper with high quality ink reproduction. It is only recently that any interest has been shown in these cards. Now they are being appreciated for their print quality, however, the prices are low. This allows a collector to have some good turn of the century printing and remain on a strict budget.

This introduction to art, with a capitol A, led to new ideas in home decoration, broader use of color, and a better understanding of what went with what. The postcard brought high quality art into the home of the working class man for the first time.

Collectors today may be frustrated by the lack of information about a particular artist that they admire and collect. It must be remembered that when an artist almost exclusively designed postcards during the Golden Age, this was considered commercial or disposable art. It has only been recently that the art community and collectors have recognized the true value of this work.

If a postcard artist did murals, posters, portraits, or important commissions, his history has been set down for todays researchers. If the artist created a lasting character, such as: the Kewpie, Mickey Mouse, or Happy Hooligan, his name has been recorded in many books. But, the artist, no matter how good, who quietly created volumes of work for only one or two publishers of postcards, is usually lost in the cracks of art history. Good design is good design. Collectors shouldn't be as concerned with where a postcard artist was born, studied, or who he married, as collecting his work for its quality.

Once you have identified an artist that makes your heart sing and have accumulated his work, it is time for further research. It is difficult to see the entire picture with only a card or two. When you have a quantity of the artist's work collected, it can be determined which publisher he worked for most often, the location of this publisher, the copyright dates, and other useful information. Then, a search of copyright records becomes possible.

Many collectors create checklists of the postcards by one artist or publisher. One individual usually does not own all the cards on the list. The entire group of collectors gain knowledge and insight into their interests by sharing information with other collectors. The lists tell the number of cards in each set, a brief description of each card, and the series numbers.

These lists, just by recording what has been seen, help collectors find out what cards they are missing. If you collect Ellen Clapsaddle and realize a card carries a Suffrage message, that may help you find the card in a dealer's stock. Chances are the card will be

filed in the Suffrage category or in an album marked *Better* material, not under Clapsaddle.

Early children's books, found at Antiquarian book fairs, are an excellent source of identifying unsigned cards. The title page identifies who illustrated the work. Many of these books had color illustrations reproduced on postcards.

The Golden Age of postcards ended with World War I. While many postcards were designed in America, most designs were shipped to Europe for printing. The German and Austrian printers created outstanding work for a very reasonable cost. The color process was better and cheaper even with the cost of the transatlantic trip back to America.

Remember, most picture postcards retailed for one cent each. European publishers recognized the large American market and created designs exclusively for export, such as Halloween, Thanksgiving, Labor Day and Fourth of July postcards. The largest English publisher, Raphael Tuck & Sons, created many cards for the American market, but even Tuck used European printers. This is printed on the postcards: *Printed in Germany*, or *Printed in Austria*.

It should be noted that, after W.W. I, there are many collectible postcards. Each decade has had something to offer in terms of style or social history. The 30s and 40s saw an exclusive American process called *Linens*. These cards have textured paper that resembles linen fabric. The air brushed designs leave a very romantic impression of that era.

Following that period was the use of good color photography that realistically recorded the social and political history of the post World War II era. Collectors should remember that in 50 years the postcards of today will be as collected as those of the 40s. Surely the postcards of the 40s will be just as collected as the cards of the Golden Age. In these modern times, much of our history is

lections of postcards in museums that can be studied. These include the Jefferson R. Burdick Collection of Postcards at the Metropolitan Museum in New York City and the Curt Teich Archives at the Lake County Museum near Chicago, Illinois. Usually, museum collections are available, for viewing, to researchers only by appointment. The Teich collection also has a public exhibit.

Although it is rewarding to concentrate your collecting interests to one publisher, artist or geographic area, it is difficult not to add a card to your collection just because you love

"MONK, I'VE NO EARTHLY CHANCE IN THIS PICTURE POSTCARD COMPETITION. LOOK AT THE SIZE OF THAT CHAP'S ALBUM!"

being recorded on electronic media; radio, television, film, compact disks, and computers. The picture postcards with young people in punk hair styles, messages of ban the bomb and nuclear power, antivivisectionist and the equal rights amendment will all be desirable to collectors.

There are several vast col-

it. It may be unwise to limit yourself to just one category. The more diversified the collection the easier it is to sell to a dealer.

There are many postcard clubs and dealers in the United States. To identify a club or dealer near you, purchase an *Annual Guide* from the *Postcard Collector*. §

16

Preservation

Collecting vintage paper creates some special concerns regarding its preservation. If you like to keep antique photo or postcard albums complete as they were originally assembled, you will have even more problems. The real disadvantage is that most early albums were made of inferior green or black construction paper that leaves a residue on the postcard corners. If a top quality album was used, this slick paper didn't move or breath leaving heavy indents on the postcards called album marks. Cards should be removed from these old albums.

The major enemies of paper are fire, water or humidity, dirt, sunlight, mold, and bugs. To secure vintage paper from fire, only a vault will do. Water is a major enemy, even as humidity. Dealers should always cover their stock with plastic sheets when leaving a show. Often sprinklers have gone off, roofs have sprung leaks and guards have spilled coffee, only to have the stock saved by a plastic sheet.

If you are investing large sums of money in postcards for your collection or dealer's stock, fireproof file cabinets or a vault is advisable. Collections can be protected in a safety deposit box, which is cool, dry, dark and theft proof.

Separate each item with acid free paper, glassine or Mylar to prevent ink transfer. Stand cards on edge when possible, stacking causes damage to embossing and mechanisms.

Keep humidity at 50-65 percent; too low and the paper becomes brittle; too high and microorganisms grow. The temperature should be under 75 degrees. Heat causes faster chemical deterioration.

Sunlight is a great destroyer of paper. If you wish to display your framed collection, do not place the items in direct sunlight. Instead, display them on interior walls away from natural light. When having your items framed, be sure to request *museum mounting*. If the shop doesn't know what you are talking about, select another store.

Nothing should ever be done to paper that cannot be easily undone. If an inventory must be kept, do it in pencil. If the item needs to be secured to album pages use only stamp hinges, photo corners with clear Mylar tops, linen or paper tape. Never affix any kind of tape to the front of your postcards.

Dealers use plastic sleeves and album pages. Collectors should not, unless they are sleeves or pages of archival quality. A dealer's stock is constantly changing and cards are seldom in contact with this Poly Vinyl Chloride (PVC) storage system for long.

This PVC material will cause chemical damage to antique paper if left for long periods of time. In addition, postcards that are not in a humidity controlled environment risk water damage from condensation forming inside of the sleeves. This can be seen at outdoor flea markets. When items in plastic are exposed to the sun, they heat up creating condensation that can cause irreversible water damage.

Before you panic about the storage of your postcards, remember they have survived nearly 100 years in old deteriorating postcard albums. They probably will survive many more years with just a reasonable amount of care, but only archival protection will preserve them indefinitely. §

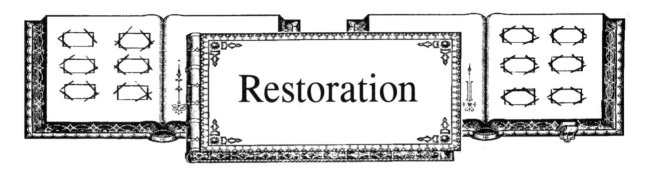

Restoration

Most postcards are usually very sturdy and can exist for hundreds of years. Yet, some are thin or soft resulting in creases or tears. All postcards are affected by fungi and bacteria plus the added strain of modern chemicals in the air. To increase the life of postcards, store them in a dark or low light, cool, and moisture free environment.

When restoring postcards begin by examining them with a strong light. Place the light at a forty five degree angle and examine the surface. This will let you see dirt, foxing, tears and creases. Use a magnifying glass for closer examination. Then, place the bright light beneath the postcard. Check for thin spots in the paper where problems may occur if not handled properly. These thin spots are caused from having been glued into an album and then improperly removed.

When you examine your postcard microscopically you will notice it is not smooth. It has a bumpy surface that collects dust from the air. To help preserve your postcards remove this surface grime. Do not rub hard, as this dirt can be abra-

sive and cause further damage.

Using a Professional Dry Cleaning Pad, purchased at an art supply store, produces the best results. This bag can be gently rubbed over the entire surface after examining the paper under light to identify trouble spots. The aim is to improve the condition of the paper; not create more damage. If you do not have the patience for this type of work, it is better to leave it alone than to make it worse. Always be sure to test a small area on the back before jumping right into the cleaning process.

All postcards are slowly being destroyed by the chemicals and sizing in the paper. The sizing material attracts moisture allowing the growth of microorganisms. Foxing, light brown spots, is usually the result of mildew.

Bleaching can often remove foxing. Foxing is not just on the surface, but embedded in the paper. It will not erase. First, rest the postcard face down on a piece of heavy blotting paper. Then, apply the bleaching solution only to the discolored area. Cover the area with blotting paper and a piece

of glass. The purpose of the glass is to apply pressure to the blotting paper, therefore, a ½ inch thick piece of glass is best.

A variety of bleaching agents can be used. Hydrogen peroxide, not more than 2% solution, Oxalic acid crystals dissolved in distilled water, or for very hard to remove stains, use a solution of sodium hypochlorite. Regular household laundry bleach is about a five percent solution of hypochlorite. It should be diluted with distilled water, using two quarts of water to each cup of bleach. Think carefully before attempting this procedure. If the foxing is spreading, it may be necessary. Always practice on a postcard of little value.

Only immerse postcards into a bleach solution if absolutely necessary. The bleach may greatly affect colors. Always place the postcard to be bleached on a clean piece of glass before immersing. This gives you a solid surface to remove the wet item from the bleach solution and the rinsing steps. After total immersion, pieces should be rinsed with distilled water until the bleach has been removed. Then, place in a bath of distilled water for 30-60 minutes. Practice your technique on a piece you are willing to sacrifice in the name of experimentation. Over bleaching will turn the paper chalky. Examine postcards before you purchase them for this chalky residue indicating it has been over bleached.

Insects also can cause damage to postcards. If the small dark spots appear on the surface of the postcard, they might be fly specks. Before bleaching, try removing these spots with a fingernail or a knife. If you find silverfish or other bugs, you must fumigate.

Grease stains are sometimes a problem on postcards. A warm iron and blotting paper will remove the grease, but chemicals are necessary to remove the stain. The chemicals required to remove these spots are dangerous. The two used are carbon tetrachloride, whose fumes are poisonous, or benzine, which is flammable. These are lightly applied to the spot before ironing. Always use in a well ventilated room. To be safe, just remove the grease and live with the stain. It is advisable to stop short of perfection rather than go beyond repair.

Wax stains are a problem on Christmas postcards because of the candles used on vintage trees. First, remove the surface wax with a razor blade. Place a blotter under the card and apply a thin coat of turpentine over the wax stain. Do not become alarmed if the paper turns clear or images from the reverse side show through. These will return upon drying. Cover the postcard with a blotter and press with a warm iron.

The most common kind of damage to paper is creasing. Pressing can remove creases. First, slightly dampen the creased area with distilled water. Cover with a blotter and press with a warm iron. If this is not enough, soak the creased area with distilled water and place between two blotters. Place weights on the blotter postcard combination, letting it dry slowly for several hours.

When postcards or tradecards have been glued into an album, care should be taken in their removal. A warm water bath works most of the time. Before drying, carefully feel the glued area for any sign of a sticky surface. It is easier to correct the problem at the initial removal stage than later after it has dried. If any hint of glue remains, rinse the paper with warm water until all traces of glue are removed. Then, soak it in distilled water for at least 30 minutes. This final rinse removes residues left by the glue. Place wet paper items between blotter pages and press with weights for a slow careful drying process.

Repairing tears is another major problem for collectors. Never do anything that cannot be undone. Never, never touch the edges of a tear. The slight-est amount of skin oil, even from clean hands, can become the magnets that will attract dirt to the tear's surface causing a visible line of discoloration. Most glues have harmful chemicals in their composition that will cause deterioration later. Never use cellophane tapes, masking tape or rubber cement on vintage paper. It would be better to leave the item torn. Paper tapes or linen tapes, purchased from art supply stores, have the necessary characteristics for repairing tears. These tapes have water soluble glues as their base. If the result is not satisfactory, they can be removed by simply wetting.

If a good deal of repairing is to be done, you can make an inexpensive glue at home that is safe for vintage paper. Measure out four heaping tablespoons of rice starch into an aluminum or enamel pan. Measure two cups of cold distilled water, adding only enough to the starch to make a thick creamy base. Boil the remaining water and add very slowly to the creamy base over a moderate heat, always stirring. This should be used immediately and not stored.

Cut mulberry paper to cover the tear completely, leaving about a half inch border around the tear. Apply the glue in a thin layer on the mulberry paper first, then affix the paper to the postcard. Mulberry paper can be purchased at most art supply stores. §

Framing

If you wish to have a frame shop do the work for you, be sure they understand museum mounting. If they do not, chose another shop.

Museum mounting uses hinge mounts, acid free mats and back boards, and never applies any type of tape to the front of the postcard. Ask what type of tape is to be used to affix the postcard to the mat. If the reply is *Scotch tape* or *Masking tape,* run, don't walk out the door. This response means the shop does not understand museum mounting or archival preservation.

If they say, linen tape or mulberry tape, ask to be shown how they do it, or an example of work you can examine outside the frame. If they are not willing to explain their procedures, don't trust that they will take extra care with your vintage paper item.

Most frame shops have a backlog of two to three weeks. Ask how they are going to store your original postcards until they work on the framing order. You can request, that they record all measurements and you return with your vintage items the day of assembly. Don't

be afraid to ask questions!

There are many "do-it-yourself" frame shops in metropolitan areas that are very helpful in showing you how to obtain the look you want.

To frame any vintage paper item requires careful measuring. Measure twice, cut once. That rule saves mat board, framing stock, time and frustration.

Always start by measuring the item to be framed. Measure the print or postcard carefully, subtracting ¼ inch from your outside measurements for the mat to overlap. For example, if the postcard is 3½ inches by 5½ inches, start with the measurement 3¼ inches by 5¼ inches. This allows an eighth of an inch overlap on each edge. Then, decide how much matting border you wish. Small prints, like postcards, generally have 2-3 inch borders, medium (11 by 14) 3-4 inch borders, and larger prints something proportional to the work.

If you have a vertical postcard, it is a good idea to have an extra ½ inch of mat border at the bottom, with the top and sides of equal measurement. An item 3¼ inches by 5¼ inches should have a mat with an out-

side dimension of approximately 7¼ by 10¼ inches.

If you wish to use commercially pre-built frames, start with the frame's outside dimensions, such as 8 by 10, and subtract the 3¼ and 5¼ from each dimension netting 4¾ inches. This is divided equally on both sides of the final mat border.

Do all the math on paper when trying to fit your print and mat into an existing commercial or antique frame.

Never have a mat on an 8 by 10 print of less than 2 inches on each side. The mat color or size should not overwhelm the print. However, if an 8 by 10 print is just a Victorian face and you want the vintage paper item to be the focal point in a room, don't hesitate to put 6 inches of mat on each side. Use a soft natural color that compliments the background of the print and the wall coloring of the room. If you are going to use a very large mat on a small piece keep the frame very simple. Don't use a large wide floral gilded frame with a huge mat and a busy print.

All vintage paper items should have a mat or space bar between the surface of the print and the glass of the frame. A mat adds the most professional look to a framed piece. The mat should be 100% rag paper or, at the very least acid free. Never put the colored side of a mat next to your postcard.

The mat has two parts, the solid back board to which the print is hinged and the front board that has a window to allow the art work to show. The back board is hinged to the front frame board with linen tape across the top. The paper item is attached to the back board with linen or mulberry tape. Use paper hinges that are lighter than the paper to be framed. If the item is dropped or severely jarred in shipping the hinges will tear away, not the print. Hinges are easily replaced, the vintage paper item is not.

The hinges are applied to the top of art work to be hung. Never apply tape to all four sides of a print. The art work needs to breathe, expand, and contract with the changes in humidity.

To attach the art work to the back board, first place the work on the back board so it is properly centered in the mat window of the front board. Carefully lift the front board out of the way holding the art work in the center. Using four pieces of tape (museum mount-

ing type only) attach two pieces at the top, with half the tape applied to the back of the print and half extending beyond the top of the print. Then, to fasten the print to the back board tape over the two pieces of tape.

Apply the first two pieces of tape to the back of the print in a vertical fashion. Apply the second two pieces of tape horizontally. Each hinge forms a T

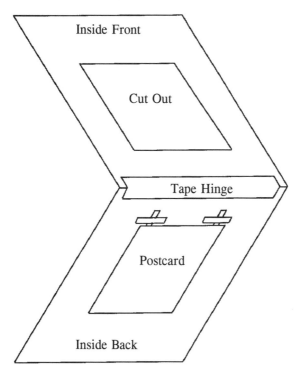

Inside Front

Cut Out

Tape Hinge

Postcard

Inside Back

with the vertical stem attached to the art work and the horizontal cross bar attached to the back board.

You may make your own hinges using mulberry paper and rice starch glue, but, use the glue sparingly. To facilitate easy removal in the future, it is advisable to apply the glue only to the center of the mulberry paper.

Once the mat is assembled,

whether you cut it yourself or purchase it commercially, you are ready to frame the work. An artist's fine hair brush is excellent for removing lint or animal hair that may have landed on your mat. You may use glass, non-glare glass or Plexiglas in your frame. The disadvantage of Plexiglas is that it fogs if cleaned with a window cleaner and scratches easily. However, it is light weight and ideal for large pieces. The disadvantages of non-glare glass are that the surface texture of the glass often distorts the art work and it is twice the cost.

If you insist on hanging your vintage prints in sunlight, non-glare glass should be your choice. The glass should be carefully cleaned on both sides.

Never put glass directly on vintage postcards or valuable art work. Moisture gathers under the glass, encouraging the growth of microorganisms that will attack your vintage paper. Ventilation is the key word. Allow air circulation between the glass and the print. Allow air circulation between the back of the framed print and the wall by applying small pieces of felt or cork to the corners of the frame. This also protects the walls from scratches when you hang the framed item. §

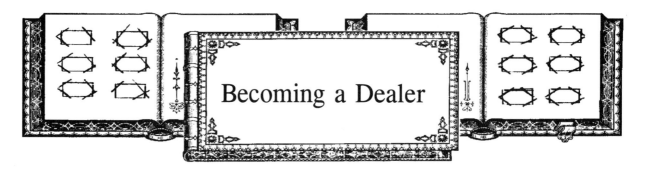

Becoming a Dealer

There are many reasons why a collector becomes a dealer. Collector's interests change or other times, space and finances force collectors to sell their cards. When collectors retire, they often look for a way to continue their interest in their hobby and travel. Collectors occasionally buy cards they feel are under priced through their collecting years with the idea of someday becoming a dealer. Whatever the reason for becoming a dealer, there are certain things you need to know to be successful.

L. - Comment faire lorture ?

PRICING

When pricing cards use a soft pencil and mark each card near the stamp box. Place each card in a protective sleeve, if the cards are going to have considerable handling, be displayed at a flea market, or are more than $1 each.

If the cards are going to be sold in 25 cent and 50 cent boxes, this is not necessary. However, it is advisable not to mix boxes at one show. In other words, take all 25 cent cards to one show and all 50 cent cards to the next show, unless you are willing to price all the cards in one group or another. Typically the cards will get mixed from box to box at a show.

Some dealers choose to price their postcards by placing a white sticker with the price on each sleeve. This helps a collector looking at the postcards, since they do not have to turn over each postcard to find the price. This reduces the wear and tear on the postcards. However, when using this method, be sure the postcards are marked on the back in pencil. On occasion, some buyers will switch postcards to a sleeve with a lower price.

SORTING

It is a common practice when establishing a dealers

L. - Si jations a Paris ?.

stock, whether using professional boxes or shoe boxes, for the cards to be filed *behind* the category divider. If you do not do this, collectors will have your cards misfiled very quickly. Even a sign saying "file in front" will not correct this problem!

Dealers, after each show and sometimes during a big show, have to check for filing errors. Collectors are often in a hurry or distracted and will file them incorrectly. A vertical divider, with the word *marker* printed on it, helps to stop this problem. Sometimes collectors hide prospective purchases in another category, thinking they will come back. If they don't, the cards remain misfiled causing loss of sales.

Postcards are sorted by state, city and occasionally county. Some dealers find it

helpful to place a large colored dot sticker folded over the top of plastic sleeves that contain real photo views. With this system, the photo cards can be filed behind the city dividers, yet spotted quickly by the collector of only real photo views. If this is too much work, sort real photo views separately.

There are many categories for topics. The more topics there are, the easier it is to find a card. Don't have a topic divider for just two postcards, or you will be carrying more weight in dividers than in postcard stock.

DISPLAYING

Better postcards, especially those cards more than ten dollars each, are best displayed in an album. There are postcard album pages that accommodate three, four or six cards.

If you are going to feature sets, the six pocket page allows a complete set to be displayed, but the album is larger and heavier. The common practice is to use four pocket pages. The top loading pages are preferable. Side loading pages let the cards slip out causing damage to the material you are trying to protect. The three pocket pages are side loading and not often used. Be sure the cards fit the pages. Forcing a card into a pocket causes creasing.

The cards can be placed back to back in the album pages with stickers on the pages to display the price. Otherwise, the client has to remove the cards to find the price on the back, each time taking a chance of damaging the card. Be sure the price is on the back of the postcard in pencil.

Pricing album pages is best accomplished by putting stickers in the lower corner and pricing in pencil. When the card is sold, another card can be put in its place and repriced simply by erasing the original price. If you choose to mark your stickers in ink, removing the stickers each time, a sticky residue may build up. This can be removed from album pages with a product called *Goo Gone*,

available at most discount stores.

Albums suggest you have better quality cards. It allows a collector to look quickly at the cards without damaging the material. The use of albums cuts down on theft. Some dealers use 3 to 5 inch thick albums to create a weight that thieves can't easily remove. This ties up a lot of salable stock as each person looks at the album. Breaking down the large album into three albums allows three collectors to look, increasing your chance of sales.

It is your responsibility as a dealer, to stop *album stacking*. This occurs when a collector removes several albums at once. This is unfair to collectors and yourself. When this happens, remove the extra albums saying, "I will hand these to you one at a time."

Because of the high table costs and theft, many dealers

place their albums on backup tables. This causes added work, but gives you a more direct contact with the customer. If a client asked for Halloween cards, you might suggest looking at your Winsch album or your Clapsaddle album. They may also contain Halloween cards. If the albums are in front, the collector may quickly look at Halloween and move on, missing your other stock.

If you have some outstanding cards, it is to your benefit to have these on display. This can be done on small easels, open albums, or under glass. The lightest weight display material is Plexiglas, which scratches easily. It is advisable to attach a piece of colored mat board under the Plexiglas with clear, wide tape. This prevents the cards from slipping as customers lean on the glass. It can enhance the presentation by using black or gray mat board. This type of presentation can eliminate the need for a table covering.

Plexiglas, cut 8 to 14 inches wide by 28 to 30 inches long, makes good vertical display pieces. The narrow width allows you to open the display to show cards without disturbing every customer in your booth. By hinging the display glass with clear wide tape on the long edge, they open easily. The mat board backing provides a protective board between each sheet of Plexiglas when stacked, to prevent scratching.

TABLE COVERINGS

Table coverings usually add to your display, but avoid blocking your view of the floor. Do not drape table coverings lower than four inches from the top, if you are selling from behind the table. If you are positioned in front of the tables, floor length covers look good. Most postcard shows have dealers

Emma, y La Dèche.

behind their tables.

This makes it easy for a thief to place a bag, purse or newspaper on the floor into which they will drop cards. Dealers have caught thieves because they could view the bags on the floor. If you find an open bag on the floor, ask the client to close their bag or suggest they place it behind your table. If a customer gets offended and quickly moves on, consider yourself lucky. You probably averted a thief.

Table covers are required to be fire retardant. Fire in-

spectors will light matches to your cloth to check. They do not take your word for it. When purchasing material check that it is naturally flame retardant, washes easily, and doesn't wrinkle. Bright colors attract attention, while black makes a good background.

If you prefer another type of fabric, call your local fire station for the formula for fireproofing material. It is easy, but generally leaves the fabric very stiff.

SUPPLY BOX

You will need a box to carry many odds and ends. The size can be determined by what it contains. The following supplies always seem needed when least expected; scissors, duct tape, masking tape, Scotch tape, paper clips, thumb tacks, extra sleeves, extra dividers, extension cords, extra light bulbs, converter plugs (from three prong to two), change, tax forms for recording resale numbers, receipt books, pencils, erasers, magic markers, pens, bags or envelopes. Don't forget to include show cards of the next shows where you will be selling, and checklists of your or your customers wants. General first aid and medicines are necessary, such as: aspirin, Band-aids, cough drops plus addresses and phone numbers of dealers. Don't forget the kitchen sink, or the next best thing a few handy wipes and a roll of paper towels.

INTRODUCTION

All this may seem silly. But, if you use lights for your display, it won't be worth the time carrying them if the bulb burns out or the cord won't reach. Often these cords must go across aisles to reach plugs and must be taped down with duct tape. If you get in the habit of carrying $10-50 in change in your supply box, you won't have to be dashing to a bank just before the show opens. It will surprise you how often a collector will set a drink on the glass. You should immediately remove it and wipe the area of moisture. Scissors are great if a sign needs to be cut for your hotel door, or trimming threads from your table cloth. Magic markers can

VI. - Qui veut des Cartes postales ?

make quick "sale" signs or new "markers" for the boxes. Pen-

cils for pricing and pens for writing checks both seem to vanish, so carry several of each.

Bags or envelopes with your name and address on the outside are useful. Not only is this good advertising, but if a customer looses his cards they will be returned to you and you may know to whom they belong. It is a good habit to write a customer's name on the bag as you hand them the cards. This helps you know your customers names and makes the cards returnable if lost.

PICKING A SHOW

After pricing, preparing your display materials, making your supply box and generally getting organized, it is time to pick a first show.

Do you have enough cards? You should fill at least one table with boxes or albums. The dollar value of your stock should be high enough to cover all expenses, cost of the cards and leave a profit. For example, if you only have $1,000 retail in stock your sales probably will be about $100. Is that enough? It could be, if you have very little invested in the cards, are eating and sleeping at home and paid $15 for your table.

The first show should be

close to home to cut your expenses. Local clubs usually sponsor shows near home. Therefore, you will know many potential customers by name.

Start slow and listen to other dealers and customers. If you hear grumbling about your prices, check other dealer's stocks for similar cards. Are you over priced? If you have a rush of dealers at every show, buying great numbers of your cards, your prices are probably too low.

If you can price your cards to sell to dealers, you will be guaranteed a good show. This means buying right or settling for a smaller profit margin. Dealers are usually your biggest and most consistent buyers.

The postcard shows throughout the United States are listed, by date, in both trade papers: *Barr's Postcard News* and *The Postcard Collector*. If you have just purchased a postcard stock without having attended a postcard show, attend at least one show without setting up, so you can see how it works.

Postcard show table rents vary greatly. Small local shows may be as low as $25 per table. Well advertised big city extravaganzas may be as much as $300 per table. The difference is the number of collectors that attend and usually the amount of money those collectors are willing to spend.

When paying higher rents,

The Encyclopedia of Antique Postcards

25

it is important to know whether the tables are six or eight feet. Also, ask whether a back up table is provided or if there is space for you to bring a card table. Another two feet of selling space can make a difference in total sales.

Check to see if promoters have obtained special room rates for dealers at the host hotel. This can save costs. Check with other dealers for a preferred hotel when the show is held at another type of facility. It is important to ask whether dealers will be setting up in their hotel rooms the night before a show to sell. This has become common practice at some places, such as: Wichita and San Francisco. Don't miss this added selling or buying opportunity.

Before picking a show, talk to other dealers and check the volume of show advertising. See if the show chairman has a waiting list. A waiting list usually means a demand and, therefore, a good show. If you can rent a table the week before a show, it can mean the show room is large or that they have not filled the show.

If you are going to be vacationing in an area, it might be a good time to try a show, since you would be paying the travel expenses anyway.

When picking a postcard circuit try to do several shows in a one week. For example,

you could do South Bend one weekend, Chicago the next, and because Chicago is a Friday/ Saturday show, Indianapolis or a flea market on Sunday. That is three shows in ten days. The days between should be used

VII. Les affaires marchent.

for scouting out new material or seeing private collectors. To make this a business, you must work.

Hotel time is good for pricing, sorting and filing recent purchases or calling customers to remind them about the show. If there is a postcard club, attend a club meeting with your cards or use rosters to invite other collectors to your hotel room.

For example, in the above scenario, on Wednesday between shows you could go to

Davenport, Iowa, (two hours away) and invite the Black Hawk Club members to buy at your hotel. Postcard invitations can go out before your arrival notifying clients where you will be staying. Be sure to tell the front desk they can give out your room number to anyone inquiring. This is not advisable when traveling alone.

SHARING A SPACE

A good way to get started at an established show, is to share space with another dealer. Who is willing to share the space? The most likely dealer to share a space is one that needs help. This could be a dealer that rents four tables at every show and needs assistance. The dealer may be willing to sublet half a table in exchange for helping with customers. It is a good way to learn.

Others who need help, might be the elderly. These dealers often like the social contact a show gives them, more than the monetary rewards. They may share a space if you are willing to load and unload their stock. Dealers who are alone may want someone to share a table, so they can have time to shop, go to the rest room, and get something eat. All aspects of sharing a space should be discussed before the show.

26

INTRODUCTION

SELLING OUT OF POCKET

First, you should make sure your cards have a market and are priced fairly. This can be done by *selling out of pocket*. Always check with the show chairman first, to see if it is allowed.

When selling out of pocket, a few rules must be followed. First, your customers should be friends or other dealers. Never offer what you have for sale to a collector sitting at another dealer's table. The dealer has rented that space and will be greatly offended if you try to interupt or sell to his customers.

Selling out of pocket is a touchy proposition at best, but can be done if care is taken not to upset anyone. The best situation is when you are a collector trying to dispose of cards. If you find cards you wish to add to your collection in a dealer's stock, you can offer to trade for cards you have with you.

You can go to a dealer, from whom you have purchased material, to see if he wishes an opportunity to buy it back. You can contact collectors in the show aisles, suggesting they look at your stock after the show or in the hall, but not in the showroom during show hours.

MAIL ORDER

If you don't have enough cards to set up at a postcard show or don't want to do that much work, you can sell your cards through the mail. Prospective customers can be obtained by reading the want ads

VIII. - Y n'faudrait une boutique

in the trade papers. Or you can place an ad in the trade papers asking for want lists. Running a mail auction in a trade paper also will get you a list of mail order clients.

Once you have your customer list, you must establish a business procedure. You can send the actual cards or photo-copies to clients. The first reduces the amount of time between mailing the cards and receiving the money, but it has drawbacks. Do not send any cards through the mail without a written request signed by the customer. Unsolicited merchandise does not have to be paid for or returned by the client. Some dishonest people use this as a way of obtaining free cards.

Many dealers prefer photocopies. If the client is not interested or does not respond promptly, you are free to send photocopies to another customer. This method keeps vintage postcards out of the mail. It is rare for a customer to take everything you send.

When the customer returns the copies of what he wants, with payment, you can fill his order. The customer should have return privileges on any card not meeting his standards.

It is your decision whether the dealer or the customer pays the postage. Most dealers require the customer to pay postage both ways. The best method of sending approvals is to enclose a self addressed packing container for any returns. This guarantees the materials will be properly packed when returned. Other-

INTRODUCTION

wise, customers may send expensive cards back in a regular envelope without packing.

To increase your chances of selling all cards, include a net price for each card and a reduced lot price for the entire group. If the reduced price is attractive enough the client will take duplicates, to use later to trade.

AUCTIONS

Mail auctions are another way to be a dealer. These can be done individually, printing your own catalog, or through a trade paper (see Sources).

Mail auctions are a great way to build a mail order client list. If someone bids on a certain type of card, chances are they are interested in obtaining

♦ IX - Les "Docks de la Carte postale

more of that type of postcard.

Each trade publication can send you a detailed instruction booklet on conducting a mail auction. The basic rules apply to all trade publications and should apply to any private auction.

The first step is to gather the cards you wish to sell by auction. The average price of advertising each postcard in a trade paper is $2-5 each, depending on the length of the description. Therefore, if you want to sell cards that would retail for $2 each, they should be grouped to increase the value of the lot.

There is an exception to this rule. If you have a large stock of two to three dollar cards and wish to obtain names of clients interested in this material, run a half page auction featuring just these cards. While the total sales from the auction will be small, it may be large enough to cover the expense of the ad. Thus, the cards pay for a half page ad, advertising the type of cards you have for sale, and you build a mail order list.

If you want to sell inexpensive cards in an auction without picturing them, leave the descriptions vague, such as: 100 Easter greetings. That way you can fulfill according to the bid. For example, if you receive a bid for $10, you can ship 10 cent Easter greetings, if you receive a bid of $200 you can send $2 Easter greetings. This will gain you the most money for your advertising dollar, but you must have an very extensive inventory to fill all requests.

If you wish to picture cards in your auction, choose cards valued at least $20 each. To save description time, pick cards in the best possible condition. It is easier to type "mint" after a description than list every flaw. If the card is not mint, it is important to build your customer confidence by describing every fault.

When doing your descriptions, pretend you are describing the card to a blind person. With the small black and white images that appear in the trade papers, it is almost the same. Paint a visual picture of each card in the reader's mind.

List major colors, point out details that cannot be seen in the ad, reprint titles, captions or verses. It is important to include information about the back; divided, undivided, used or unused. If information about the publisher or series number is known, it should be included. Perhaps your customer, from that information alone, can decide if it belongs to a set he is trying to complete.

When estimating the price, keep the estimates realistic or even low, to encourages bidding. High estimates discourage bidding. Remember this is an auction. For you, as a dealer, to get the best price you need several bidders. This is most successful if you accept phone bids on the closing date of the

mail auction.

Each dealer must decide if they will reveal the high bid to the phone bidder. Many reliable auction houses feel it is an auction and you have the right to know the high bid. When revealing a bid, the auction house requires a specific increase to accept a higher phone bid. Often it is 10 per cent over

X - Après fortune faite.

the high bid. This protects the mail bidders from being scooped by a phone bidder increasing the high bid by 50 cents.

When you receive bids through the mail assign a bidder number to each client. By numbering the bid sheets as they arrive, you can later determine who was the first bidder if two customers bid the

same amount. The first bid received is considered the winner. If clients wish to bid by phone, record their name, address, and phone number and assign a bidder number, as if they bid by mail.

Your bidding sheets will have a lot number with notations that look like fractions after each lot. For example, Lot 5..15/12..36/22. The first number is the bidder number, the second the amount bid. You can tell at a glance bidder 36 is high on lot 5 with a bid of $22.

After the auction closes, send invoices, deposit checks, and ship the postcards. It seems simple, but the process is time consuming. From writing descriptions until the end of the auction, is usually six to eight weeks. The closing date of the auction is generally three to four weeks after publication. §

The ten card illustrated set was printed in France. It tells the story of a young boy deciding how to make his fortune in life. His first decision is to go to Paris, where he starts his business of selling a few postcards out of his pocket. This business grows until he has a large shop and becomes wealthy.

ATTWELL

WHEN YOU DO GET A LITTLE BIT
OF LUCK, HANG ON TO IT.

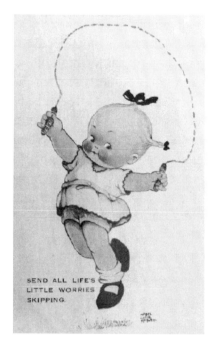

SEND ALL LIFE'S
LITTLE WORRIES
SKIPPING.

LUCK AT LAST—HE LOVES ME!

FINKS WE MUST HAVE BEEN DOIN' THE TANGO!

I LIKES YOU VERY MUCH, AN' I'M SAYING "IT" WITH FLOWERS!

EASTER GREETINGS

CHEER UP! THERE ARE STILL
A FEW BRIGHT PATCHES!

Faut pas voir la vie en noir!

30

Mabel Lucie Attwell was an English illustrator who has infected the American collectors with a desire to own her charming postcards and prints of children. Her main publisher, Valentine and Sons, reported that she produced 24 designs each year. Often, one of these designs would sell a half million copies a month.

Attwell postcards were exported to almost every country in the world. Commercial success of this kind was only partly explained by the appearance of her cherub-like children. Attwell explained it in a newspaper interview when she said, "I am mixed up with children, but I draw mainly for adults: the suburbanite, the mother, the country gossip, the young married couple, the shop girl, the flapper, the grownup. I see the child in an adult. Then I draw the adult as a child."

The appeal of many cards is the slightly suggestive message. The captions were the starting point for Attwell, according to *Strand Magazine* in 1936. She said, "In fact I never put pencil to paper until I have found a title that satisfies me. Sometimes I'll have discarded twenty or thirty titles..."

Attwell was born June 4, 1879 in London, the ninth of ten children of Augustus and Ann Attwell. At an early age, Attwell escaped into the world of art, yet, the talents of her siblings in music and art over-whelmed her ability. When, at fifteen, she said she had submitted drawings to a publisher, her family laughed. But, they were accepted.

Attwell was not a good art student because she didn't like classical drawing. She met her husband, Harold Earnshaw, at St. Martin's School of Art. He was a gifted draftsman in pen, ink and watercolor. They married in 1908. In 1909 she gave birth to the love of her life, her daughter, Peggy. She became the model for many Attwell illustrations. Her first son, Peter, was born in 1911. Brian was born in 1914 and died at the age of 20. Attwell was married for 28 years when her husband died.

In 1910, she left her drawings with an agent, who sold them all. She received commissions for posters, advertisements and books. Next Attwell worked for Valentine and Sons illustrating postcards, calendars, greeting cards, booklets, shopping lists, plaques and jigsaw puzzles.

When Attwell worked for Raphael Tuck her postcard images appeared both signed and unsigned even for the same image.

Her first annual was published in 1922, by Partridge and Company, later by Dean and Son. They were published every year from 1922 to 1974, though she died in 1964. The annuals produced after her death were taken from earlier work.

She illustrated the covers, did both black and white and color illustrations, and wrote stories and verses.

Merchandising of the Attwell image continued with china figures made by Shelly Pottery, and rubber dolls modeled from Plasticine. The dolls had names like *Snookums*, *Girlie*, *Mabel Lucie*, *The Toddler*, *Little Happy* and *Diddums*. When there was an exhibit of her dolls produced by Chad Valley Toy Company at Harrods, Attwell sent her maid to rearrange the dolls and cut their hair.

In 1937 and 1938, Princess Margaret commissioned Attwell to do her personal Christmas card. The nurseries of Princesses Elizabeth and Margaret used Attwell china. The Queen gave Prince Charles a set of nursery china in 1949.

During World War II she moved out of London to escape the bombings. Her work became less fashionable, but she was never short of work. In 1943, she started a cartoon strip for the *London Opinion* called *Wot a Life*. She moved, with her son Peter, to Cornwall in 1945 where she died in 1964. §

MABEL LUCIE ATTWELL

AVIATION

This set, published by Raphael Tuck of England, is a prime example of great design featuring early aviation. This set is numbered 406 in America and series 9 in Europe. Tuck did oilette series of early aircraft, including *In the Air*, *British Lighter than Air Craft*, *Famous Airships*, *Ships of the Sea and Air*, *Airships*, and *Famous Aeroplanes*.

Most collectors prefer real photographic postcards or cards featuring commercial aviation. We must remember that aviation was in its infancy with only thirty licensed pilots in America at the turn of the century.

Newspapers spurred this early fascination with planes through contests with prize money as high as $10,000 for flights between certain cities.

Postcards and souvenirs of these early successful flights are rarely found.

Postcards sprang up to record large events such as the International Aviation meet in Chicago, Illinois, in 1911. The postcards with least value in the aviation category are the cards issued by museums, because they were published in such great quantities. §

The Bleriot Monoplane

The Spherical Balloon

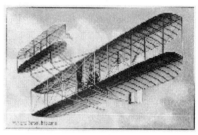
Wright Brothers Biplane

The Antoinette Monoplane

Zeppelin

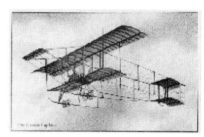
The Farman Biplane

R.P.E. Monoplane

La Republique

A.V. Roe Biplane

M. de Lesseps' Channel Flight

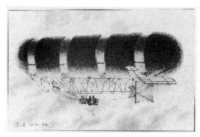
Nulli Secundus

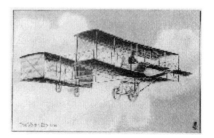
The Voisin Biplane

BACHRICH

M·BACHRICH

Bachrich created Art Deco style women on postcards. His use of limited color on all black costumes in this series reflects the confidence of this artist. Titled, *The Dance*, each figure seems frozen in a moment of time. §

<table><tr><td>La
Danse</td></tr></table>

The Encyclopedia of Antique Postcards

33

BAKST

Leon Bakst was a pseudonym for Leon Rosenberg. Bakst was his father's name before he was adopted. Born in Grodno, Russia, May 10, 1866, Baskt always claimed St. Petersburg as his birth place.

Bakst grew up in Russia when great hardships were imposed upon the Jewish people, except for a few elite who lived in St. Petersburg, such as many gifted artists and musicians. It was because of this antisemitism that so many Jews went to live

31st Exhibition of the Secession, 1908

in France or Germany.

Bakst studied at the Academy of Arts in St. Petersburg until he was censored for producing a canvas depicting biblical characters as Jews. His ambition was to be the greatest artist in the world. He drew constantly on any piece of paper, napkins, bills, menus, or business cards. He said these were nothing, but signed every one in full signature, perhaps

practicing for when he was to become the world's greatest artist.

Contributing portrait drawings to the *World of Art*, until 1904 when it closed, Bakst went on to draw illustrations for *Apollo* and *The Golden Fleece*.

He was a stage designer as early as 1902, but these works went unnoticed. The first of Bakst's theatrical masterpieces was his work on, *La Fee de Poupee's*. The theme of the

ballet was a toy shop and the new designer received recognition with the resulting work issued on postcards. This set of twelve colored postcards, issued in an envelope designed by Bakst, was sold to benefit the Red Cross. The ballet made a name for Bakst.

By 1910, Bakst's name dominated the Ballets Russes giving him international fame. In England in the 1980s, an

exhibit called *Spotlight* featured a four century tribute to the Royal Ballet sponsored by the Victoria and Albert Museum. This exhibit of ballet costumes included several of Bakst's designs.

The most noted costume was for the Swan, worn in 1907 by Anna Pavlova in St. Petersburg, Russia. It was a classic tutu of off-white silk. The shoulder straps and front of the bodice were covered with layers upon layers of snow white goose feathers, creating the look of a bird. Stiff overlaying panels formed the skirt. Feathers covered two outspread wings. The top of the skirt was of fine silk net with sequins. At the center of the bodice was a large green jewel, a sight to be remembered.

Bakst's postcard work is often overlooked. He did sets of theatrical costumes and a series for the Ballets Russes in 1908.

He died in France, December 28, 1924. §

БАКСТЬ

Л.БАКСТЬ

Л.Бакстъ

BAKST

BASCH

Arpad Basch was born in Budapest, Hungary, in approximately 1873. He was a successful painter and commercial artist doing illustrations and graphic design for books. He studied in Budapest with Karlovsky, in Munich with Hollosy, and in Paris with Bonnat and Laurens. He returned to Hungary in 1896.

His art credits include many books, almanacs and Hungarian magazines. He was the art director of *Magyar Genius*.

His postcard art is limited to a few sets. There is a ten card series of women of different nationalities, series no. 785 of cities, large and small views, and several decorative cards. This set of six women is often called female warriors. It bears no publishers name, but was copyrighted in 1900. Each card is signed Basch Arpad.

These chromo lithographic postcards are rare and highly sought after today. Basch died in 1944. §

BASCH ARPÀD

BEARS

This is a terrific example of a set of postcards telling a story. When the teddy bear became popular with Teddy Roosevelt, postcard publishers couldn't wait to express this fad on cards. These paper items are highly collected today.

This series depicts the rivalry between a doll and a bear. This well dressed Victorian child was probably the first on her block to have a teddy bear, and was anxious to show him off with a buggy ride.

She removed the doll to the step and filled the carriage with her new teddy bear. The upset doll whispers her plot to the nearby goat. The goat was probably already attracted to the mohair bear. As the story progresses, the goat inches his way toward the teddy bear, quickly grabs the bear and runs. The doll throws her arms up in delight. The child, in a heartbeat, reverts *Back to the old Love*, her doll.

While each individual postcard is colorful and well designed in its own right, the complete set is more desirable and valuable. T.P. & Company of New York, New York, published this set. §

BERTIGLIA

Aurelio Bertiglia was born in the 1890s in Turin, Italy. He was a self taught illustrator who worked from the age of fourteen creating postcards for German and Italian publishers.

He was prolific and his artistically created children are recognized by their saucer like eyes on large round heads that sit on foreshortened bodies. Besides cute children, Bertiglia drew cards about the social history of the times.

This propaganda set features Italy conquering Ethiopia. The sign on the wall dated October 19, 1913 and signed by General De Bono, translates loosely to "People of color, listen and know about the unfortunates, the flag of Italy will liberate you from your land of bondage and oppression."

The set shows Italian soldiers kicking the leaders out, breaking the chains and shackles on the legs of the common man, and feeding the unfortunate children. Then, they raise the flag of Italy and the Ethiopians all bow down as Italy repaints the Ethiopian map in the colors of the Italian flag (green, white and red).

Bertiglia was an illustrator, caricaturist, fashion designer, painter and did musical scores and publicity graphics. §

Other Examples of Bertiglia's Work

This set of billiard cards, published by Raphael Tuck of England, appears with a French Tuck back or a JVA back. The cards with the JVA backs were commissioned from Tuck, at the turn of the century, by J. Vlieger of Amsterdam, thus JVA. The JVA cards feature the Tuck easel logo on the front. The artist signed the cards.

These postcard designs were found in quantity in a European warehouse in the late 1970s. They are usually in mint condition. This is definitely a set to pass if not in excellent condition, because they are available. However, it is amazing how quickly collectors absorbed the warehouse stock. This kind of find should never

bother collectors or dealers. If the images are desirable, any card in mint condition will sell and is worth owning.

Billiards refers to two games, pocket billiards or pool, and billiards. Pool is played with 15 numbered balls. Billiards is played with three balls, one red and two white. This set is billiards. §

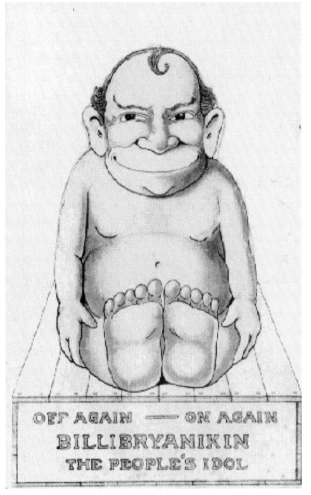

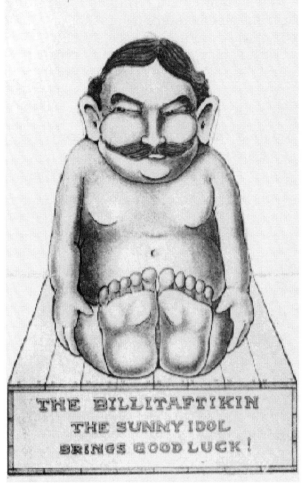

Illustrated here are, two political and one regular, Billiken postcards relating to Florence Pretz's good luck character. With both Bryan and Taft sharing the first name of William, it was a natural fit to slip their last names in after *Bill*.

Pretz patented her Billiken image on October 6, 1908. As an art teacher and illustrator, she received a seven year patent for her design, but the name Billiken is not mentioned. The Billikens were manufactured in a great variety of material by both the Billiken Jewelry Company and the Billiken Company, both of Chicago.

*I am the Source of Luckiness,
Observe my twinkling eye-
Success is sure to follow those
Who keep me closely by.*

The character was a symbol of happiness and luck, and was said to drive the blues away. A unique feature of the Taft and Bryan postcards is that they have been die-cut to form an easel much like the Kewpie Klever cards.

When the Billiken craze hit the country, Blanche Ring sang *The Billiken Man* in a hit musical comedy, in New York. A large doll manufacturers, E.I. Horsman, made two different styles of dolls. Although nearly a quarter of a million dolls were sold in the first six months, the doll's popularity was short-lived. §

BOILEAU

Philip Boileau had formal art training at the Academy of Milan, where for four years he studied traditional Italian portraiture. Boileau said he wanted a profession that "involved the very minimum of possible human effort, intellectual, manual and otherwise." That is why he decided to become an artist.

Luckily, art came very easy to Boileau and he became successful.

Boileau's mother, Susan Taylor Benton, was the youngest daughter of Missouri Senator, Thomas Hart Benton. His father, Philip Gauldree de Boileau was a French diplomat. After art school, Boileau traveled extensively, meeting expenses with promises against his inheritance.

When his father did die, he soon consumed the one-eighth share after spending six years traveling around the Riviera. He immigrated to America where his brother, Benton, was living in Baltimore, Maryland.

KNG Number 8010

Link's Modern Business College
BOISE, IDAHO

Osborne Company, New York

Philip Boileau

The years he spent in Baltimore were to heal the wounds of the death of his first wife, a Russian singer. He then moved to Philadelphia, Pennsylvania for a short time. While there he met and later married Emily Gilbert, who was to become the model for most of his later illustrations.

Boileau moved to New York where he had attended school as a child. He did not set the city on fire with his art. In fact, he couldn't get any of his work published. So, he self published his first illustration, *Peggy,* to prove that America was ready for his style. Boileau copyrighted the *Peggy* head on November 11, 1903.

Later, Boileau painted, *Sweetheart.* This 1905 endeavor was Boileau's favorite painting of his second wife. They were married in New York on October 9, 1907. Emily was 21 and Boileau was 43. The press considered Emily "one of the most beautiful women in America."

Boileau's first studio in New York was on Fifth Avenue. In 1910 he bought property on Long Island, where they spent the summers. He was an avid gardener and loved to cook the evening meal for friends and family.

After his early self published picture of *Peggy,* Boileau received a few commissions of illustrative work and for a set of postcards for the National Art Company. These are Boileau's earliest postcard work and were poorly printed, but managed to get his name before the public.

In 1904, he did another design for a postcard published by the National Art Company. It was later used on the 1908 Osborne calendar, titled *The Debutantes.*

His magazine cover designs first appeared in 1905 for *The Sunday Magazine* for Associated Sunday Magazines. He continued to design covers for this group until 1916. This work brought his cover girls into millions of American homes and led to work for Hearst and Reinthal & Newman.

Boileau did a total of 34 cover designs for *Saturday Evening Post* and many others for *Pictorial Review*, the *Delineator*, *Collier's*, *Success*, the *Housewife*, *People's Home Journal*, *Ladies' Home Journal*, *Ladies' World*, *McCall's*, *Woman's Home Companion*, *Southern Woman's Magazine*, *Holland's, Every Week*, and *War Cry*. He did covers from 1906 to 1917.

Reinthal and Newman reprinted on postcards most of the *Saturday Evening Post* and *Sunday Magazine* covers. Reinthal and Newman issued postcards on both regular paper stock and matte stock. The matte cards, called the watercolor series, are harder to find.

His rarest material is the postcards published by Osborne Calendar Company, Raphael Tuck, Taylor & Platt, and unidentified European publishers. The rule of thumb is, if it is not Reinthal and Newman, it is scarce. Boileau did about 200 different postcard designs.

With no children of his own, Boileau used the children of Clarence, Emily's older brother, as models. He often used the four children in his art work from 1911 until his death.

Boileau very wisely registered 141 copyrights of his work. This way he, not the publisher, decided if an illustration could be reprinted in another form.

Boileau's illustrations appeared on blotters, at least one book dust jacket (*Contrary Mary* by Temple Bailey), china plates, vases and pitchers, beer trays, wooden plaques, and even shirts and socks.

Boileau's death on January 18, 1917 marked the end of an era and the beginning of America at war. Emily remained a widow for 34 years. Boileau had prepared her for life by letting her travel alone in Europe and starting a career on stage.

Boileau reported, "Unless there are children, marriage is no more an absorbing occupation for a woman than for a man... the man who is afraid of granting his wife the liberty for pursuing a career that he himself demands, fears not wife, but himself... He is not sure of himself. He is an old husband and unworthy of his wife. He deserves to loose her." §

Maurice Boulanger is best known for his illustrations of cats and rabbits. The postcards feature animals doing human activities and, if dressed, it is only in hats. The series of portraits of cats, published by K.F. Editeurs, Paris, have them in big bonnets or top hats.

Boulanger's cats always have very triangular expressive eyes in bright greens and yellows. His style is often confused with that of Louis Wain.

Most of his postcard work is not signed, but when signed, it is either a small monogram of MB or a full script signature. The full signature is found most often on postcard designs that feature rabbits.

Rapheal Tuck published this set, series number 122, titled *Humorous Cats*. The set has a divided back and was used in 1908. This and his months of the year set, also by Rapheal Tuck, are among the most collected. §

BOY SCOUTS

The Boy Scout ranks in the United States today do not relate directly to the ranks on the Raphael Tuck series of postcards. The Cub Scout ranks of Wolf, Bear and Webolos were established in 1930 as were the Boy Scout Ranks of Tenderfoot, Second Class, First Class, and Star, Life and Eagle.

Each postcard from the Raphael Tuck and Sons, London, England, series, *The Tiger*, *The Lion*, *The Wolf*, *The Bear*, *The Owl* and *The Eagle* features a call of the animal or bird and a significant color. The color stated for each symbol is also reflected in the border color of the postcard. §

Tuck
No. 9950
Our Boy Scouts

This is the Life—
Your Gink

A home run for this Gink

Love thirty for this Gink

O, the sky blue sea
Is the life for me—
Your Gink

George Reiter Brill was born in Allegheny, Pennsylvania, in 1867. He died, at the age of 51, on March 6, 1918, in Florida. His unusual cartoon style, as in the Ginks, was published by the Rose Company of Philadelphia, Pennsylvania, in 1915.

Brill's egg-shaped people engage in many human activities like sailing, baseball, golf and tennis.

Ginks wrote often and were very disappointed when they did not get replies. For example, *I'm a Gink you owes a letter 2* or *I'm the Gink what wants to know why you ain't wrote?*

Only two postcards of the set feature more than one Gink. They are the postcards, *This place is full of Ginks* with three characters and *All the Ginks are doin' it* featuring a couple. This last postcard has the only female Gink.

All others feature a male in a stovepipe top hat, without trousers, but with multi-colored jackets. He sports a bow tie and stiff white collar. The ties are either white, yellow, red, blue or striped. This sixteen postcard set originally sold for a penny each.

While the most popular and collected of the Brill postcards, the Ginks are not the only postcards Brill created. In 1907, he designed a set of cards that feature roller skating.

These postcards have a small red heart in the upper right corner and are signed. Rufus Hill copyrighted this set. Hill was a member of the firm, Edward Stern and Company of Philadelphia, Pennsylvania.

In 1911, Brill designed a black and white set of postcards for the Rose Company, Philadelphia, Pennsylvania, celebrating Leap Year.

Brill was most noted for his cartoon work for *Life* magazine and his books, *Rhymes of the Golden Age, Andy and Ignoramus,* and *Paperweight Owl.* This delightful cartoon work is easy to find. §

BRILL

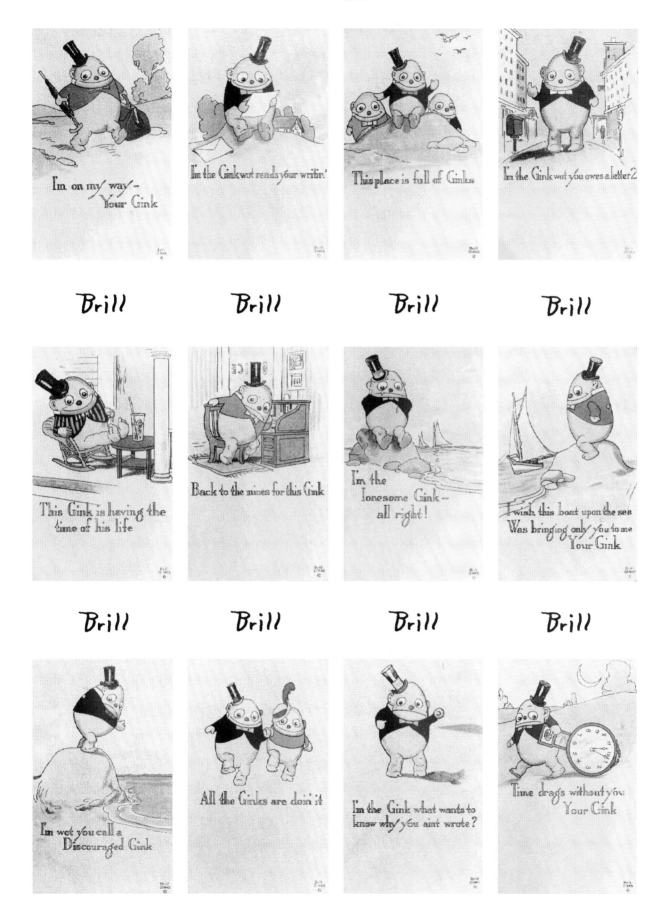

Tom Browne was born in Nottingham, England, in 1870. He attended St. Mary's National School until the age of 11, when he took his first job as an errand boy. By age 14, he had an apprenticeship with a printer.

He first used his cartoon skills entertaining his friends with caricatures. They encouraged him to do cartoons for the newspaper comic pages.

When he was 17, Browne sold work to *Scraps* for pay equal to 3 months of his regular wage. This encouraged him to attend art school in Nottingham with the idea of making his fortune in London.

After two years of preparatory work, Browne went to London, only to be met with hard work and few rewards.

Finally, he created a front page comic strip called *Weary Willie and Tired Tim*. It was an instant success. Browne's biggest break was being published in *Punch*, which led to many commissions. Davidson Brothers commissioned Browne to create over 900 original postcard designs. They held an exclusive contract on his card designs.

The 400 postcards, pub-

lished by Tuck, Valentine, Wrench, Hartmann and Pasco, were taken from illustrations which appeared in books, magazines and newspapers. Many of these are unsigned.

By age 26, the Royal Academy accepted his work. In 1898, he was made a member of the Royal Society of British Artists and, in 1901, a member of the Royal Institute of Painters in Watercolor.

In 1904, he visited America and created cartoons for the New York *Herald* and the *New York Times*. In 1906, he returned to the States and worked for the *Chicago Tribune*. These visits led Browne to create series for Davidson Brothers about America. These are the most desirable of his cards. They are *Baseball Illustrations* and *American Life*. The *American Life* cards have captions for the American market and appeared without captions for the English market.

Browne died of cancer in 1910 at the age of 39. §

Tom Browne

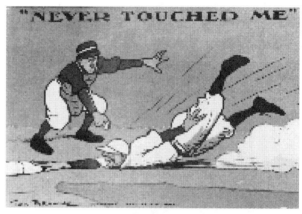

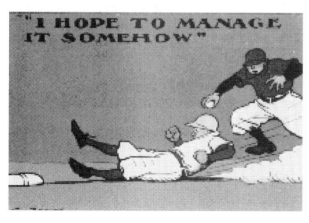

Tuck Number 666 - *Little Sunbeam*

York and Saalfield Publishing Company of Akron, Ohio.

It was not until Brundage was 32 years old that she married William Tyson Brundage, a painter. Six years older than Frances, they were well suited for each other. You even find early illustrations signed Will and Frances Brundage. William died at age 74 and Frances lived to be 82. They lived in Washington, D.C., and New York, but spent many summers at Cape Ann, Massachusetts. It was traditional for many artists to escape the sweltering heat of the city.

Her earliest postcard work was for Raphael Tuck Publishing. These early undivided back cards of large heads of children are scarce. The association with Tuck lasted from 1900 to 1910, when she left to work for the Samuel Gabriel Company of New York, New York.

This change in publishers altered her art style. The Brundage Gabriel children were more like normal children, running, playing and getting into trouble. The Tuck Brundage children were portraits of Victorian girls. The Gabriel postcards are much easier to find than the Tuck.

She signed her cards with either a monogram or full signature. §

On June 28th, 1854, Frances Brundage was born to the Rembrandt Lockwood family in Newark, New Jersey. Her father was artistic, being an engraver and architect, but he left the family when Frances was a teenager.

Brundage earned money doing drawings and paintings for the books of Louisa May Alcott and illustrations for plays of Shakespeare. She has many books for children to her credit. Her *Baby Book* is a real treasure. Brundage books were published by Samuel Gabriel and Sons Company of New

BRUNELLESCHI

Umberto Brunelleschi was born in 1879 in Montemurlo, Italy. He studied at the Academy of Fine Art with Giuseppe Ciaranfi and Raffaello Sorbi.

He worked as a cartoonist for magazines like *Le Rire*, *L'Assiette au Beurre*, and *Frou-Frou* under the name Aroun-al-Rasic. He exhibited his paintings in Paris, gaining a commission to work on the *Journal des Dames et des Modes* and the *Gazette du Bon Ton*. These fashion illustration magazines were among the best in Paris.

BRUNELLESCHI

He illustrated the books, *Contes du Temps Jadis* and *La Nuit Venitienne*, and designed costumes and sets.

After the war, he worked on large stencil plates creating pochoir designs that were highly successful from 1925-1929. He published his postcards from 1915 to 1935. Brunelleschi did postcards on military subjects, women, and jobs.

He inspired such Italian postcard artists as Busi, Corbella, Meschini and others.

Brunelleschi died in Paris, France, in 1949. §

BULL DURHAM

Bull Durham Smoking Tobacco

America

Mexico

Sandwich Islander

Japan

Russia

Iceland

Spain

Germany

Ireland

The Scotchman

Italy

Egypt

52

BULL DURHAM

Durham, North Carolina

China

India

South America

Turkey

Switzerland

Holland

Morocco

Panama

Philippines

Canada

Alaska

Brazil

Asia

England

France

Portugal

Australia

Orange Free State

North Pole

South Pole

Bull Durham's Trip Around The World
FREE a Handsome Souvenir Postal Card
with each 5 cent bag of Bull Durham

This thirty three postcard set is a very desirable advertising group published to be given away by the Bull Durham Smoking Tobacco Company of Durham, North Carolina.

Each postcard is numbered. Postcards 31 and 32 look identical, but one card is titled *North Pole* and the other *South Pole*.

An advertising poster, announcing the card premiums, featured the complete set of postcards and was displayed in stores selling the tobacco product. §

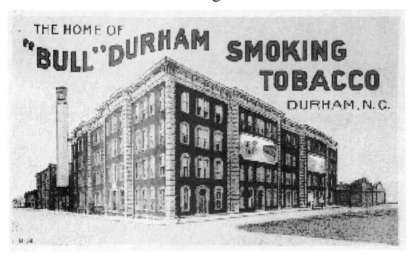

54

BYRRH

The 113 postcards in the Byrrh advertising set feature the work of the very best postcard and poster artists during the European golden age of cards. Each card in the set is attributed to the artist in a cut line on the front.

Byrrh was a leading producer of Tonic water containing quinine. Quinine, a bitter, extracted from cinchona bark, was used in the treatment of malaria.

The most important card to American collectors is the card designed by Raphael Kirchner. This unique card cleverly used the name Byrrh in reverse, mirror image and normal to form a wallpaper design behind the lovely women. La Petit was the only artist to create two cards.

The cards all feature the tonic water, and a line saying it is good for your health and contains quinine. Each card is very individualistic in style. Some are boldly colored, others muted shades. They feature men, women, children and even bears and monkeys drinking Byrrh tonic water.

Some are in cafes or in homes. The Leon Selves' postcard shows a police officer chasing a man in a checkered suit who has stolen the tonic. Croize's card has a nursing mother, with baby, drinking the water. §

Only Horizontal Card

Envelope

Harrison Cady and Thornton Burgess created the most exciting children's literature with Cady doing the pictures and Burgess the verse. They did books, magazine stories and articles for newspapers from 1911 to 1960.

Burgess was born in Sandwich, Massachusetts, January

14, 1874, where there is now a Burgess museum. He is best known for his 200 children's books and over 900 stories.

Cady, born June 17, 1877, is best known for his newspaper comic strip, *Peter Rabbit*. It only appeared on Sunday from 1920 to 1948 but resulted in 1,459 episodes. He died, 1970.

Cady created over 3,000 illustrations for over 30 magazines and newspapers. His forte was the fantasy world of animals which appeared on 48 magazine covers, in 450 items for *Life* and nearly 200 items each for *People's Home Journal* and *American Boy*.

The Thorton Burgess books, published by Little, Brown Company, were the *Mother West Wind Series*. The

first four books were illustrated by George Kerr, the last four by Harrison Cady. The stories before 1912 do not carry a Quaddies trademark, those from 1912 to 1927 do carry the trademark.

The first book in 1910, *Old Mother West Wind* included: *Why Grandfather Frog Had No Tail*, *How Reddy Fox was Surprised*, *Peter Rabbit Plays a Joke*, *How Sammy Jay Was Found Out*, and *Spotty the Turtle Wins a Race*.

The 1911, *Mother West Wind's Children* include *Danny Meadow Mouse Learns Why His Tail is Short* and *Why Hooty the Owl Does Not Play on the*

CADY

Green Meadow. The 1912 book, *Mother West Wind's Animal Friends,* features the same characters. The fourth book, *Mother West Wind's Neighbors,* 1913, added the stories *Unc' Billy Possum Arrives* and *Happy Jack Squirrel's Stolen Nuts.* When Harrison Cady illustrated book five, in 1915, the ten characters in the postcard series had already been established in the first books.

In 1915, Burgess wrote stories for the newspaper about how Peter Rabbit started a Quaddy Club for his animal friends. The Quaddy Club was formed for the love and protection of the "Little Children of the Forest."

This ten card set is copy-righted and licensed by Burgess, drawn by Cady and published by the Quaddy Plaything Company of Kansas City, Kansas. Each postcard is signed, H. Cady. The back of the card says "This card entitles — (name) to membership in the Quaddy Club... If you'd be a real, true Quaddy, Send a card to everybody." §

1A. *Yes, Ain't I cute?*
1B. *Hurray! Hip, Hip, Hurray!*
1C. *I love to hop an' skip*

2A. *Rig-a jig-jiggy, I'm Mama's*
2B. *I'se Dorothy C, Gay as can be*
2C. *This little girl with golden*

3A. *If all the sea was Campbell's*
3B. *When my ship comes in*
3C. *Your Summer Girl*

4A. *I've scanned the far horizon*
4B. *The naughty, bad*
4C. *The wind blows East*

5A. *A sad, sick boy in our town*
5B. *It's an ill wind that blows no*
5C. *If I could drive an aeroplane*
5D. *For Vigor and Vim*

6A. *On with the dance*
6B. *Little Mary, light and airy*
6C. *The hop step, the drop step*
6D. *Oh! My! but I am happy*

Numbers 1 - 6 With Known Verse Variations

7A. *Good Gracious! nearly six*
7B. *My best girl's a Suffragette*
7C. *Votes for Women, yes, you*
7D. *She won me for her happy*

8A. *Walking down the golden*
8B. *I'm drest like angel*
8C. *Earth would be a paradise*
8D. *I'd like to be an angel*

9A. *A joyous heart, A pretty face*
9B. *If you would train, To run*
9C. *Does he run a marathon?*
9D. *In a Hurry, Hurry, Skurry*

7B & 7C Rarest of All

10A. *My What a grand scrumbunc-*
10B. *Oh, my, how good I feel*
10C. *The lily's perfume's lovely*
10D. *The scents of Araby*

11A. *Around and 'round I blithely*
11B. *I gaily whirl with every girl*
11C. *There are many funny dances*

12A. *Ali Baba's Treasure*
12B. *I dropped my dolly in the pot*
12C. *At the end of the rainbow*

Numbers 7 - 12 With Known Verse Variations

The Encyclopedia of Antique Postcards

CAMPBELL'S KIDS

13A. I declare! says Fanny Fair
13B. What tender thoughts
13C. When Sally Sweet walks
13D. Each day I find some

14A. As sun and soil and silver
14B. Dancing Daisy, plump and
14C. For Campbell's Soups
14D. Campbell's Soups each day

15A. A forceful Campbell boy
15B. Curve them over how you
15C. Now, you out-field chasers
15D. These soups instil such

16A. Bye, lo, bye my baby
16B. Delicious soup, my heart
16C. I weep for you, my Dolly
16D. O, weep with me my Dolly!

17A. A maiden coy, a grocer's boy
17B. A rose from the garden
17C. Here comes the lad who fills
17D. The nourishment fine

18A. I am a pirate bold
18B. I am young Robinson Crusoe
18C. I boldly seize such soups
18D. Sing Ho! for the C on my

Numbers 13 - 18 With Known Verse Variations

19A. *Each Campbell kind just*
19B. *My rosy cheeks and*
19C. *This luscious soup just hits*
19D. *These soups so fine, folks*

20A. *Boo! I Say to needless care*
20B. *I represent surprised content*
20C. *I'm Jack-in-the-can*

21A. *All day long I sing my song*
21B. *I'm gladdest when I sing of*
21C. *Where'er I roam*
21D. *O come with me in the*

22A. *Bright can, come near*
22B. *Mary's lamb loves*
22C. *Leave me not, dear Campbell*
22D. *Dear can, I weep lest fate*

23A. *A sweet contemplation*
23B. *Campbell's soup so softly*
23C. *That fragrance rare of*
23D. *O, Campbell's! What a dainty*

24A. *O, Hark! O, Hear!*
24B. *How I rejoice to hear*
24C. *A song of Campbell's Soup*
24D. *A plate of Campbell's Soup*

Numbers 19 - 24 With Known Verse Variations

CARR

Erin Go Brag

A King for a Day.

After the Parade.

Following the Crowd on St. Patrick's day.

Impish little creatures playing children's games and getting into trouble were the forte of American cartoonist, Eugene Carr. The bug-eyed children have monkey-like faces, bright red noses and oversized shoes. These tough kids smoked cigars, tied a pail to a puppy dog's tail and put firecrackers in an old man's pocket. The streets and alleys were their playground and an assortment of puppies always accompanied the kids.

Carr was born in New York on January 17, 1881. He died in 1959. Much of Carr's work reflects the carefree hours children spend entertaining themselves. Perhaps this is because Carr went to work at the age of nine. He worked for the *New York Recorder* running errands, but spending every spare moment in the art department learning the craft by watching. At fifteen, he had launched his long and prolific career. He worked for the New York *Herald*, the *World*, the *Evening Journal*, the *Philadelphia Times*, *McClure,* and King Features Syndicates.

The list of comic strips he worked on or created is extensive, although only a few were popular. He started with *Lady Bountiful*, a modern fairy tale which Carr created for the New York *Herald* in 1904. In 1906, he produced for the New York *World* a strip called *Nobody Works Like Father*. In 1913, Carr took over Rollin

Kirby's *Metropolitan Movies*. It became Carr's most notable feature and was popular enough to be reprinted in book form under the title, *Kid Cartoons*. There were dolls, china, and other premiums made of the Gene Carr kids.

If Carr had stayed with one cartoon feature, instead of being restless, perhaps he might have become more popular. He did a host of titles including: *All the Comforts of Home, Buddy, Uncle Crabtree, Phyllis, The Jones Boys, Father Romeo, Willie Wise, Ready and Caruso,* and *Flirting Flora.* Carr freelanced for *the Saturday Evening Post, Redbook, Collier's,* and *Liberty*.

During the early 1900s Carr created a delightful group of 51 postcard images.

Rotograph, St. Patrick's Day Series FL 187-192 from 1906, the cards are as follows: *Sh-s-s-s-sh* (187), *Erin Go Brag* (188), *A King for a Day* (189), *After the Parade* (190), *The Day the Dutch lead the Irish* (191), *Following the crowd on St. Patrick's Day* (192).

Rotograph, Comic Series FL 201-213 from 1906, the cards are as follows: *Now Jimmie run and buy me that piece of pie* (201), *Chasing the Duck* (202), *57 Varieties* (203), *Nix Kid!* (204), *Won't be home (hic) for dinner tonight!* (205), *Zhe-ee W'ot Bit Potato Bugs!* (206), *the Baby has his Father's Nose and Hair* (207), *Beauty and the Beast* (208), *Chums*

(209), *In the Good Old Summer Time* (210), *Stung* (212), *Four of a Kind* (213).

Rotograph, Mosquito Series 218, from 1906, the cards are as follows: *The Jersey Stork* (218/1), *Dan Cupid at the Shore* (218/2), *On the Bum* (218/3), *Who's on the Line* (218/4).

Rotograph, Fourth of July series 219, from 1906, they are: *What are you laughing at?* (219/1), *King* (219/2), *Nice Dorg!* (219/3), *Pals* (219/4), *The Morning After* (219/5).

Rotograph, Children's Games series 242, copyright 1907, the cards are as follows: *Baseball* (242/1), *Marbles* (242/2), *Follow-Master* (242/3), *Snow Balling* (242/4), *Snap the Whip* (242/5), *One-o-Cat* (242/6), *Swimming* (242/7), *Skating* (242/8), *Potsy* (242/9), *Hide and Seek* (242/10), *Football* (242/11), *Leap frog* (242/12).

Bergman Publishing did three Easter series by Carr. They are Series 2003, 2004 and one card 8515. The cap-

tions are as follows: Series 2003: *A Glad Easter, and Many of Them*; *A Happy Easter to You*; *Joyful May Your Easter Be*; *May this Eastertide be the Best Ever*; Series 2004: *Happy Easter may it Find You*; *Merry be Your Easter Season*; *Right Happy be your Easter Day*; *The Merriest Easter Ever*; *Through we are living far apart*; Series 8515: *When nature smiles on all*, *at Easter, may we all have a smile for her*.

The New York Sunday *World* did a reproducing card titled, *Why is father running?* The reproducing postcards were puzzle cards. To solve the puzzle a piece of paper was placed over the card and rubbed with a pencil. What appears is the Carr signature and four people throwing lemons at father with the caption, *23 for you Skiddo.* §

The Day the Dutch lead the Irish.

CAVALLY

Multiplication is vexation

Tell tale Tit!

Dame Bear made a curtsey

To make your candles last for aye

Little Ted Snooks was fond of his books

See-saw, Margery Daw

What are little Ted Boys made out of?

Ding dong bell, my Teddy's in the well!

64

As I went to Bonner

Cock crows in the morn

The Thayer Company of Denver, Colorado, published this postcard set in 1907. Designed by Fred L. Cavally Jr., the images were reproduced from the illustrations in *Mother Goose's Teddy Bears*, published by the Bobbs Merrill Company. Cavally was born in 1878 and died in 1962. §

Teddy be nimble

Little Ted Grundy

Wash me, and comb me

Nose, Nose, jolly red nose

Little Ted Horner
Sat in a corner

Rain, rain, go away

Sophia Chiostri, daughter of famed illustrator Carlo Chiostri (1863-1939), was born in Italy in 1898. She lived only six years beyond her father's death in 1939. She had one sister, Evelina, two years younger. Evelina died the year after her sister in 1945. Neither woman lived to the age of fifty.

Her postcard designs, in the Art Deco style, are highly sought after in Europe and America. Most of her cards were published in Italy. The colors are striking and the quality of printing is good. §

S
O
P
H
I
A

C
H
I
O
S
T
R
I

CHRISTY

There are nine College Kings and Queens by Raphael Tuck. The College Kings are numbered 2766 and the College Queens are numbered 2767. The rarest card is a King of Clubs for WILLISTON, numbered Tuck 2794. Williston is a private college prep school in East Hampton, Massachusetts.

F. Earl Christy designed all nine cards. While Williston is the same image as the Cornell King of Hearts, Williston is in Blue and Cornell is in red. It is assumed Williston commis-

Williston

sioned Tuck.

F. Earl Christy was born in Philadelphia, on November 13, 1883. He studied at the Pennsylvania Academy of Fine Arts.

The Christy College girls were published by Tuck, Schwerdtfeger, Platinachrome, Bein, Reinthal and Newman, Ullman, Souvenir Post Card and Illustrated Postal Card.

F. Earl Christy postcards are well designed, colorful, and usually of pretty women. §

F. EARL CHRISTY

Michigan   *Chicago*   *Cornell*   *Columbia*

Princeton   *Harvard*   *Pennsylvania*   *Yale*

CLAPSADDLE

Ellen Clapsaddle was a very prolific postcard artist. After a small amount of study, her artistic style is easily recognized, whether signed or not. Her children are the most sought after cards, though she did simple landscapes, animals, modest Christmas scenes and sampler type cards.

She designed thousands of images for postcards during her career and wrote the verse

did nearly all their published designs. However, during the war, paper and printing inks were at a premium resulting in a poorer quality product. After the war interest in postcards waned and Wolf closed in 1931.

Ellen Hattie Clapsaddle was born in South Columbia, New York, on January 8, 1865. Descendants of the American Revolution, her parents Dean and Harriet Clapsaddle edu-

artistic talent. In 1885, she returned to South Columbia where she did china painting and home decorative painting, like boudoir screens. After her father's death in 1891, she and her mother moved to Richfield Springs to live with her aunt.

In 1898, Ellen and her mother traveled to Europe at the expense of the International Art Publishing Company. Clapsaddle's mother died in 1905 and Ellen moved to New York City. She traveled several times to Europe for the company and was in Europe when World War I broke out, but friends managed to bring her back to New York.

Because of the failed Wolf Company, Ellen Clapsaddle died destitute at the Peabody Home in New York on January 7, 1934. She was buried in Lakeview Cemetery in Richfield Springs, New York, where her parents were buried. §

Ellen H. Clapsaddle

for her work. Clapsaddle worked for several publishers, including Raphael Tuck, and the International Art Publishing Company, owned by the Wolf family. In 1917, she invested her life savings in the Wolf Publishing Company and

cated Ellen in the rural schools until sending her to Richfield Springs Seminary where she graduated in 1882.

After Richfield, Clapsaddle attended the Cooper Institute in New York City for two years where she developed her

Wolf
Publishing
Series
501

Rare
Halloween

Clapsaddle Designs

Inter-Art
Series
1301

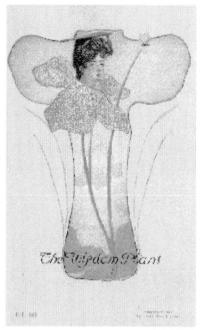

F.L. 161

F.L. 162

F.L. 163

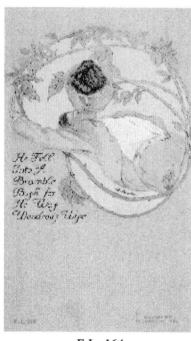

F.L. 164

F.L. 165

F.L. 166

John Cecil Clay was born on April 2, 1875 in Roceverte, West Virginia. He studied under Henry Siddons Mowbray in New York and specialized in pastel sketches of New York's famous theater and political figures. He exhibited sketches of writers, Booth Talkington, Joel Harris and Mark Twain.

Clay did illustrations for newspapers and magazines, including over 100 illustrations for *Life* magazine from 1902-1907, twelve of which were covers. Nearly all this work deals with romantic subjects.

In 1904, Clay did *In Love's Garden* and in 1905, *The Lover's Mother Goose* for Bobbs-Merrill Publishing of Indiana. *In Love's Garden* was a gift book with 37 color plates, each featuring the fantasy of

CLAY

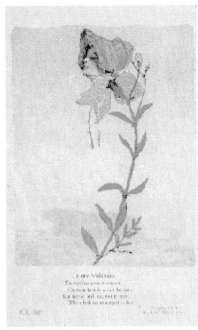

F.L. 167

F.L. 168

F.L. 169

F.L. 170

F.L. 171

F.L. 172

women as flowers. *Life* sold the book in a gift box for $3.00. He worked with Oliver Herford on four other books from 1908-1917. Clay suffered a stroke while in his forties rendering him unable to work. He died May 24, 1930.

Clay's work appears on postcards, published by Rotograph, Detroit, Volland, Armour, and a Pictorial Comedy-Snap Shot series, published in England. This featured twelve card set is often overlooked and under-rated. The postcards from the Pictorial Comedy-Snap Shot series are scarce. §

John Cecil Clay

The Encyclopedia of Antique Postcards

CORBELLA

Tito Corbella was born in 1885 in Italy. He used his wife as a model. In his studio in Venice, he created over 300 postcard designs.

His most important set features the story of Nurse Edith Cavell, killed during World War I by Germans soldiers. Corbella did several powerful propaganda sets during the war, but most collectors prefer his glamour work.

Corbella worked for International Art, Ital d'Arte, Ricordi and Stampa. He died in 1966. §

T. CORBELLA

S
E
R
I
E
S

5
3
6

Created by Urbano Corva, an Italian impressionist, these cards are successful in giving an immediate impression of the object. The impressionist's technique was to show light as it appears to the eye.

To create this effect, Corva applied small areas of intense pure color. Each card has spots of pure green, blue, or yellow, with most of the surface in earth tones. This twelve post-card set is shown with the envelope, at the right. §

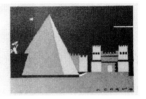

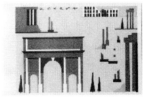

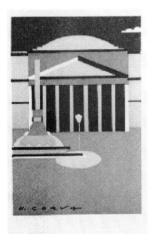

No. 1

No. 2

No. 3

No. 4

No. 5

No. 7

Advertising Postcards Numbers 1 through 16

No. 6

No. 10

There is hardly an American alive that hasn't dug into a box of Cracker Jacks, dreaming of the prize to follow. Frederick William Rueckheim first sold the mixture of molasses, peanuts and fresh popcorn from a Chicago street stand in 1871. The snack was so popular, a factory followed. From 1871 to 1899 Cracker Jack was sold only in bulk at street stands in Chicago.

The first big break for Rueckheim came when the new snack was sold at the World Columbian Exposition in 1893 in Chicago. After this event, which 21.5 million people attended, the business increased so rapidly orders always exceeded production. The name came in 1896 when one of their salesman exclaimed, "That's a Crackerjack!" That piece of Victorian slang stuck with the product for the next century. By 1908, the confection even turned up in a popular song, "Take Me Out to the Ball Game... buy me some peanuts and Cracker Jack, I don't care if I ever get back!"

In 1899, Henry Eckstein developed the wax sealing paper and moisture proof box. This allowed the product to be widely distributed.

The company claims it put the first prizes into the boxes in 1910 or 1911, but according to Alex Jaramillo, author of

No. 8

No. 9

No. 11

No. 14

No. 12

Cracker Jack Prizes, "the truth seems to be they were offered as early as the mid 1890s". Jaramillo states, "the Cracker Jack bear cards were found in the boxes... with the opportunity to complete the sets by mail, but the beginning point was the card in the box."

Another way of obtaining the cards, was to send ten side panels from boxes of Cracker Jack, or ten cents and one side panel from the box, to Rueckheim Brothers and Eckstein of Chicago, Illinois. B.E. Moreland copyrighted the cards in 1907. They and are slightly smaller than standard postcards.

The most desirable postcards in the set are number 12, the bears playing baseball, and number 10, the bears with a jack-o-lantern. East coast collectors prefer number 4, the Cracker Jack Bears sitting on the Statue of Liberty. §

Copyrighted 1907 by B.E. Moreland

No. 13

No. 15

No. 16

Of Dutch descent, Rie Cramer was born in Indonesia in 1887. She returned to Holland until she was nine.

W. de Haan published her first children's book in 1906. This book was so successful it launched an illustration career that lasted for decades. Between 1915 and 1917, she illustrated many children's literature

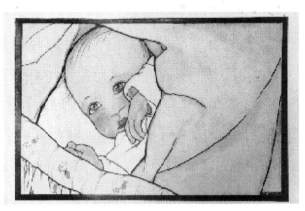

classics, like *Mother Goose's Rhymes* and *Andersen's Fairy Tales*.

Her career also extended into advertising design, fashion illustration, and the writing of plays, novels and poems.

Most of her over 200 postcard designs were reproductions of the illustrations from her books. The most famous of her books was *Spring Flower,* first published in 1914.

Cramer married twice but had no children. She died in 1977 at the age of ninety. §

RIE CRAMER

Taft's political symbol occurred in a cartoon in the Atlanta *Constitution*. A rotund Taft holds the possum, who says to Roosevelt, "Beat it! Teddy Bear, Beat It!". The caption reads, "If Teddy Bear why not Billy Possum?" The Lester Book Company reprinted it as a postcard.

While Roosevelt's mascot was the teddy bear, Taft had the possum. In 1904, Roosevelt declared he would not be a candidate for re-election in the 1908 campaign. True to his word, Roosevelt did not run in 1908, but was influential in having his Secretary of War, William H. Taft, nominated.

The first use of a possum as

Taft was inaugurated in March of 1909. Several postcards feature the possum (Taft) taking over for the teddy bear (Roosevelt). Shortly after Taft's election, Roosevelt became disillusioned with Taft's performance as President. It may have started with what is called the "Charlie Incident."

Taft reportedly said his brother Charlie had given him the Presidency. Roosevelt responded that Charlie may have provided the money, but he had given him the nomination.

Roosevelt's disappointment in Taft was what Roosevelt perceived as Taft's rebuttal of the press and his slow decision making, which led to quick compromise to reduce conflict. This clash between Taft and Roosevelt is seen in political postcards like this set, designed by Crite and copyrighted by L. Glick in 1909. One image has the possum devouring a roasted teddy bear.

By 1912, Roosevelt was so disappointed in Taft, he threw his hat in the ring again. The postcard publishers had a field day pitting the possum against the teddy bear and many cards

feature this rivalry, but none quite like these.

This twelve postcard set has deep red borders and is printed on soft paper stock, making it nearly impossible to find in mint condition. §

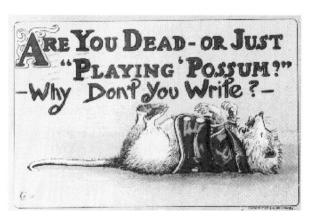

DARLING

Jay Norwood (Ding) Darling was a cartoonist for 49 years. When Roosevelt died in 1919, Darling drew Roosevelt on horseback, waving his hat and joining a procession of departed American pioneers winding their way into the distance in covered wagons. Captioned, *The Long, Long Trail*, this cartoon appeared on millions of books, calendars and reprints.

For 40 years his cartoons occupied the front page of the *Des Moines Register,* totaling 16,000 illustrations. For 32 years, his cartoons were syndicated across the United States.

He won Pulitzer prizes in 1924 (only the second given for cartooning) and in 1943. The 1943 cartoon pictured Washington, D.C., buried under piles of government reports with the caption, *What a place for a waste paper salvage campaign.*

"Ding" at Work on His Daily Portrait of Mrs. Everyman's World

Darling started his career in 1900 for the *Sioux City Journal.* Six years later, he went to work for *The Register.* In 1911, Darling moved to New York and did his cartoons for *The Globe.* Darling returned to Des Moines in 1913 saying he was unable to maintain contact with the people of America.

Darling recommended a cartoonist to take his place on *The Globe,* offering to pay his salary for six months if it didn't work out. However, Robert Ripley's *Believe It or Not* cartoons were a success.

Darling fought a lifetime battle against pollution. His first cartoon for the Des Moines paper was about soft coal polluting the city. He said in 1935, "When I first saw this state, it was like a paradise... Wide prairies, blue from flowers. The wild turkeys had not disappeared, Prairie chickens were as thick as English sparrows, the streams were full of fish. During the first half of my life, I saw them all disappear."

In 1934, Darling left a $100,000 a year job to head the U.S. Biological Survey. During his term in Washington, he increased the game preserves from 700,000 acres to 5.7 million acres. He worked to create and design the first duck stamp, that cost hunters $1.

Ding Darling's best known cartoon character was the Iowa fat farmer. Many Iowa men said they were the model, but Ding denied it. This image first appeared in 1919.

His postcard illustrations are signed with a full signature, while his cartoons and cards, reprinted from cartoons, are signed, J.N. Ding. §

Breakfast Time

DAYS OF THE WEEK

Sunday's Child is Bonnie and Good

Monday's Child is Fair of Face

Tuesday's Child is Full of Grace

Wednesday's Child is merry & glad

Thursday's Child is Sure to be Sad

Friday's Child is Loving & Giving

Days of the Week cards were common during the Golden Age. This series, signed *J.S.*, was taken from a children's book, *Polly Parson's Party, A Story for Little Tots* by Uncle Milton, published and copyrighted by Ullman in 1907. §

Ullman Manufacturing Company
Birthday Sign Series 82
Numbers 1915 - 1921
Copyright 1907

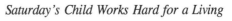

Saturday's Child Works Hard for a Living

The Encyclopedia of Antique Postcards

83

William Wallace Denslow is best known for creating the illustrations for the original *Wonderful Wizard of Oz*. He spent most of his professional life in Chicago, Illinois, as an innovator of children's book illustrations. After meeting at the Chicago Press Club, Denslow illustrated Lyman Frank Baum's first book, *By the Candelabra's Glare* with a pair of pen and ink drawings.

To his signature, the initials *DEN*, Denslow added a sea horse or hippocampus that led to his nickname of Hippocampus Dan. His experience with Asian art while in San Francisco inspired the idea of a monogram. "It is well to have a sign or totem, as my hippocampus has saved many a composition for me, and I hold him in reserve for that purpose," Denslow wrote. Nowhere is this better demonstrated than when examining the 24 color illustrations Denslow created for that first *Oz* book.

William Denslow (1856 - 1915) made comic drawings even as a small child. He studied at the Cooper Institute for the Advancement of Science and Art and at the National Academy of Design.

Earning only a meager living for six years in Philadelphia, as an illustrator for newspapers, theatrical posters and *The Theater* magazine, he went to work for the *Herald* in Chicago. He left Chicago to work in Denver and San Francisco, but returned to cover the World Columbian Exposition for the *Herald*.

Denslow left the *Herald* in 1895 and worked as a free-lance artist. Later, he designed book covers for the Rand McNally Company, creating over 100 designs, sometimes as many as one a day. In 1898, Denslow did illustrations for Montgomery Ward.

After the first *Wizard of Oz* book, Denslow and Baum had disagreements, but decided to collaborate on another book, *Dot and Tot*. The men each went their separate ways before this book was completed. Each later created their own successful books, so not much disappointment was expressed when *Dot and Tot* failed.

Denslow created *Denslow's*

DENSLOW

Night Before Christmas, Denslow's Picture Book, Denslow's Scarecrow and the Tin Man, and *Denslow's Mother Goose*. Other books feature many of Denslow's illustrations, but few postcards were printed of his work.

The advertising postcards for Teddy Bear Bread, made by the New England Bakery of Pawtucket, Rhode Island, are hard to find. The scarcity of the cards was created because a Teddy Bear stick pin was given away as a premium when returning a completed set of cards to the store. The merchant immediately destroyed the postcards.

The Denslow Thanksgiving postcards are more common, however, with such limited choice the Denslow collectors appreciate this set. It is very colorful. §

Viola Grace Gebbie was born in Darby, Pennsylvania, on October 14, 1877. Her parents George Gebbie and Mary Jane Fitzgerald lived in a large Victorian home. Her father was a successful art book publisher. Grace had two sisters, Janet, who died at the age of 20 and Margaret (see M.G. Hays), whom Grace called Peggy.

Grace drew from an early age. According to an article in the July 1912 issue of *Strand* magazine, she could not remember a time when she did not draw. The darling children she created were actually perfected from early childhood self portraits. These sketches, created while she looked into a mirror, delighted her convent school classmates, who recognized Grace in the drawings. Grace reported, "I kept on making round roly-polys, consulting the mirror from time to time. Eventually I had created a type that was as much a part of me as myself... When I thought of a career, I found I had one in just keeping alive these youngsters I had created in and from my own childhood."

When Grace was a teenager, her father died, causing the family financial distress, as well as the loss of a loved one. At 17, Grace accepted professional art assignments to keep the family going. By 18, she had a cover assignment from *Truth* magazine, but for a long time after that no magazine purchased her work.

Grace married her first husband, Theodore E. Wiederseim Jr., when she was 22 in April 1900. Her artistic break came when Seymour Eaton started *The Booklover's Magazine*. Although she received no pay, her work was in the public eye. After her first illustration appeared, New York *American*, in 1903, offered her a two year contract.

In 1904, she began her 20 year relationship with Campbell's Soup Company. She divorced her first husband in 1911 and later that year married W. Heyward Drayton III. Drayton was very wealthy and socially prominent. They had a winter home in Florida and traveled a great deal. This marriage ended in divorce in 1923. She never remarried.

With this history in mind, you are now aware that Grace's work was signed Grace Gebbie, G.G. Wiederseim, and Drayton. Her work was prolific not only on postcards, but in magazines and books written and illustrated with her sister, Margaret. She designed embroidery pieces and dolls. One of her most successful endeavors was her series of *Dolly Dingle* paper dolls, published in magazines.

Grace was a member of several professional organizations, including the Academy of Fine Arts of Philadelphia, the Author's League of America, the Society of Illustrators and the New York Art Center.

By December, 1933, Grace was poverty stricken after loosing her job with King Feature Syndicates. She wrote to Bernard Wagner, her background artist, "I have no work and am almost down and out. I have tried everything... I feel so sad whenever I look at our empty studio. To add to my agony, I lost my only dearly beloved sister a few weeks ago. So I am now all alone and poverty stricken in the heart as well as in pocket... Nevertheless, I try to keep my pug nose in the air..."

She died two years later on January 31, 1936, at age 58, of a heart attack. She was buried in Philadelphia, Pennsylvania, in an unknown location.

The signed Wiederseim cards were published by Reinthal & Newman, A. M. Davis, Campbell Art Co., Alfred Schweizer and Raphael Tuck & Sons. They appeared from 1907 until 1911 when she divorced Wiederseim and married Drayton. The Drayton cards appear from 1911 to 1916 and were published by Reinthal & Newman. The signed Drayton postcards are harder to find. This signed Drayton set, published by Reinthal and Newman, depicts the stages in a woman's life from meeting to first child, a theme used by several artists (see Fisher; Campbell's Kids). §

Love at First Sight

The Trousseau

The Wedding

The Honeymoon

First Night in their New Home

Their New Love

Rare
Raphael Tuck
Halloween
Series
#807

DUDOVICH

Marcello Dudovich was born in Trieste, Italy, in 1878. He was a painter, designer and illustrator of posters and postcards. His first commercial art work was for Ricordi and Chappuis. Dudovich did magazine illustrations for *Tlalia ride*, *Novissima*, *Varietas*, *Ars et labor*, and *La Lettura*.

In 1913, the editor of *Simplicissimus* published an art portfolio of Dudovich's sketches of lively social life studies titled *Corso*.

In 1919, the famed Lenci Doll Company employed Dudovich to do preparatory sketches of the dolls. His design talents and established illustration career added to the style of the fashions for a newly created cloth doll.

Much of his postcard work reflects the fashions and fun of the twenties. Dudovich died in Milan, Italy, in 1962. §

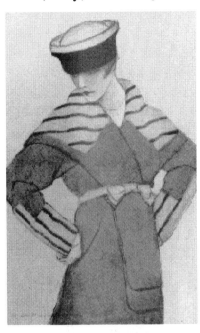

Clare Victor Dwiggins, born in Wilmington, Ohio, on June 16, 1874, and was educated in country schools. He left home at the age of sixteen to explore the world. His career as a cartoonist began when he took a position with the *Saint Louis Dispatch* for two dollars a week. Dwiggins signed his work Dwig. Collectors always refer to his work as done by Dwig.

Dwig's first postcard work was for Henry T. Coates and Company in 1902. These cards were reproduced from a book, *Whimlets*, illustrated by Dwig for the H.T.C. Company. The series numbers on the cards directly correspond to the page numbers of the illustrated book.

In 1903, Dwig started work for the New York offices of Raphael Tuck and Sons. He submitted pen and ink drawings that were shipped to England for coloring and printing. This relationship continued for many years. From 1906 until 1910, Dwig free-lanced for many publishers, including: Charles Rose, C. Marks, R. Kaplan, C. W. Anderson, Sam Gabriel, Cardinell Vincent, A. Blue, Ninon Traver and L. Gulick.

Besides postcards, he produced comic strips and panels entitled, *School Days, Tom Sawyer and Huck Finn, Nipper and Bill's Diary*, and *Ophelia*. There were many other strips, but his most outstanding one was the Sunday feature, *School Days*.

This 1910 strip greatly differed from a later panel series of the same name. The early Sunday half-pages were usually one large panel, featuring school children getting into trouble inside or directly outside their one room school. In the background their pretty teacher was flirting with various gentlemen callers.

From 1917 to 1932, Dwig produced the daily panel series with the same title. His finest cartooning work ever was in this later series. Dwig's Sunday pages, such as *Nipper* and *Tom Sawyer*, were syndicated. Late in his career he tried an adventure strip called, *The Adventures of Bobby Crusoe*, but it was unsuccessful. He returned to book illustration, which he had done early in his career, and produced work until his death in Hollywood, California, on October 26, 1958. His wife died in 1947.

Dwig was a prolific postcard artist using his wife as a model for many of his cards or occasionally his daughter, Phoebe. The Dwiggins had a son, Don.

Many of his sets contained 12 to 24 cards. They had great titles like: *Never*; *What do you know about that?*; *You need a*; *Help wanted*; *What's the use*; *The wurst girl*; *If*; *Don't*; *Smile*; *School days*; *Cheer up*; *There's a reason*; *How can you do it?*; *What are the wild waves saying?* and many more.

Copyright, H. T. C. & Co., 1902. No. 56.

Dwig's first postcard work was for Henry T. Coates and Company in 1902. The series numbers on these cards directly correspond to the page numbers of Dwig's book *Whimlets*.

Copyright, H. T. C. & Co., 1902. No. 59.

This Halloween series is not signed, but is undoubtedly Dwig's work. The colors are bright and vibrant. He skillfully created the fantasy designs. §

Published by
J. Marks, New York
Series 981

The Encyclopedia of Antique Postcards

RARE
Series Number 101
WIDOW'S WISDOM
Cardinell-Vincent Company

DWIG

BREAKFAST
IN BED
CHARGED EXTRA

RAPHAEL TUCK
SERIES
9321

RAPHAEL TUCK
SERIES II
9553

ELLAM

William Henry Ellam was an English artist who created postcard designs of animals, working for publishers like Excelsior, Faulkner, Mack, Philco, Wrench, Tuck, Stiebel, Tilley, and Woolstone.

His animals participated in human activities like those il-lustrated in the *Breakfast in Bed* series 9321 and 9553, produced by Raphael Tuck and Sons. His teddy bear postcards are highly collected, as well.

Raphael Tuck also produced the novelty puzzle postcards by Ellam, series 9684. Sold in envelopes containing a regular postcard and a puzzle, this was a technique by the publishers to create a new market for two postcards instead of one.

Generally puzzle postcards feature cities, scenes or buildings, therefore, these elephant puzzle postcards are an added delight for collectors. §

Mixed Bathing

Real Style

Crowded Out

Trunk Loads of Merry Tales

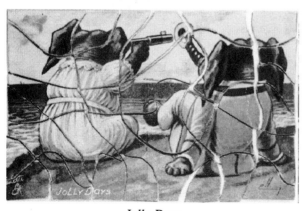

Jolly Days

Morning Exercise

96

EVOLUTION

#973 Evolution of a Farmer

#974 Evolution of Uncle Sam

#975 Evolution of John Bull

#976 Evolution of a Russian

#977 Evolution of a Watermelon into Coon

#978 Evolution of a Capitalist

#979 Evolution of a Brother

(Goat turns into fraternal brother)

#980 Evolution of an Irishman

#981 Evolution of a Baker

#982 Evolution of a Chinaman

#983 Evolution of a Butcher

#984 Evolution of a German

#985 Evolution of a Milkman

#986 Evolution of a Fireman

Evolution of an Irishman

Evolution of a Chinaman

The fourteen card (#973-986) Evolution set was clever, as well as cruel, in its melting of one image into another. The bag of flour turns into a baker, the goat into a fraternal brother, and even a fire hose evolves into a fireman.

Many depict immigrants like the English, Russians, Irish, Chinese, and Germans in a negative light, such as the Irish man evolving from a whiskey bottle or Chinese man from a laundry tub. Women were not attacked in this set but Afro-Americans were, with the card depicting a *coon* evolving from a watermelon.

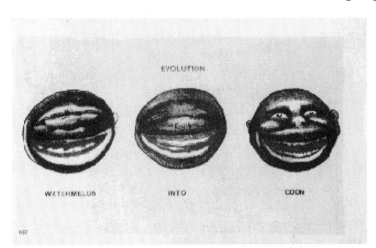

Evolution of a watermelon into Coon

This set is a good example of how postcards from the Golden Age reflected the social history of that era. Today, this type of artistic humor about ethnic groups would not be tolerated in print. Much of the same humor is spread verbally in jokes about Afro-Americans, people of Polish dissent, Mexicans and even women, through "dumb blonde" stories.

The most expensive and hardest to find of the evolution series is number 977, the Afro-American postcard. §

EXPOSITION

The beginning of the commercial picture postcard era started with the World Columbian Exposition in Chicago in 1893. The fair occupied 633 acres, had 14 major building, 42 state buildings, 17 foreign buildings and more.

The purpose of these expositions has always been to promote travel, trade and understanding between cultures. It was at these fairs that new products were introduced, contemporary art was displayed and a glimpse into the future was provided.

Most expositions were held in big cities with easy transportation routes and a ready supply of workers and attendees. Although most of the fairs were not profitable, cities wanted them for publicity.

Expositions had a special way of helping the populace escape troubled times, like war and economic depression, and step into a fantasy land of adventure and beauty. There was an added educational component buried in those pavilions of art, literature, and music. All major industries either brought their latest products to dazzle the public or set up factories in miniature to manufacture products in their pavilions.

1873 Chicago
Inter-State Industrial Exposition
1893 Chicago
World Columbian Exposition
1894 San Francisco
California Midwinter International
1895 Atlanta
Cotton States and International Exposition
1898 Omaha
Trans-Mississippi and International Exposition
1901 Buffalo
Pan-American Exposition
1901 Charleston
South Carolina Inter-State and West Indian Exposition
1904 St. Louis
The Universal Exposition or St. Louis World's Fair or Louisiana Purchase Exposition
1905 Portland
Lewis and Clark Centennial and American Pacific Exposition and Oriental Fair
1907 Norfolk
Jamestown Tercentennial Exposition
1909 Seattle
Alaska-Yukon-Pacific Exposition
1909 New York City
Hudson Fulton Celebration
1915 San Francisco
Panama Pacific International Exposition
1915 San Diego
Panama California (first year long expo)

Each manufacturer, artist or participant vied for the many ribbons, plaques and medals that were awarded. Winning these awards meant precious approvals that lasted for decades, like Gold Medal Flour.

Many expositions and fairs had a theme tied to specific historic events, like the opening of the Panama Canal, the discovery of America by Columbus, and the Louis and Clark expedition.

Most postcards issued for these expositions were view cards of the grounds and attractions. While many exposition postcards are readily available, there are always exceptions.

The Hold to Light postcards issued for the 1904 St. Louis Exposition featuring the Inside Inn are scarce. To get these postcards, you had to be a guest of the Inn. Other hard to find postcards are those issued before the fairs opened, called pre-officials.

Pre-officials were made for the World Columbian Exposition. There is only one difference between the pre-official and the official postcards. The official cards carry a gold seal and a facsimile of the signatures of the fair's president and secretary.

While town celebrations had been held for centuries, during the postcard era there were an outstanding number of such events and expositions. Because of the vast number of these events, we can see the great sense of regional and national pride.

The rural areas had state fairs; so an urban celebration usually focused on local events, like the founding of the town. The expositions held in major cities, such as the World Columbian Exposition held in Chicago in 1893, have many

postcards about the event. Only a few within each group are considered rare.

Local events, such as the *250th Anniversary of Newark, New Jersey,* are not common on postcards. These minor events had a limited postcard market, therefore, fewer cards were produced. A very colorful set of postcards represented this 1916 celebration, which lasted May through October. The strong American poster style of these cards makes them highly collectible.

Many postcards represented the Exposition of 1900 in Paris, France. The S.F.B.J. Doll Society created this set for that exposition. It features the wonderful French Jumeau Bebes or dolls from that time.

Each Jumeau doll is dressed in the height of French fashion and is participating in activities that were available at the fair, like elephant and ostrich rides. The postcard featuring children playing marbles is the

LES BÉBÉS JUMEAU A L'EXPOSITION DE 1900 - HORS CONCOURS

1900 PARIS
Jumeau
Societe Francaise
de
Fabrication de Bebes
et Jouets
S F B J

most desirable of the set. Don't pass any of these in any condition. They are rare.

Of the French dollmakers, Jumeau was one of the best. They participated in many trade expositions and their history can be traced through these fairs. Jumeau participated in the 1797 show held in the Champ de Mar, the next in 1801 and the largest in 1849. By the 1900 Exposition,

LES BÉBÉS JUMEAU A L'EXPOSITION DE 1900 - HORS CONCOURS

LES BEBES JUMEAU A L'EXPOSITION DE 1900 - HORS CONCOURS

of companies would make them more competitive with the strong German doll manufacturing industry. It was their intention to improve their merchandising and offer bigger displays at the expositions. Postcards were there to promote the cause.

At the 1900 Exposition, S.F.B.J. advertised the dolls as, "Elegant and haughty with their silken dresses, the frills of lace, the frou-frou of their

Jumeau had been included in a conglomerate called Societe Francaise de Fabrication de Bebes et Jouets that was formed in 1899 (SFBJ).

This society acquired all the important doll makers when the exposition occurred. The doll trade had been falling on hard times since the middle of the 1890s. This syndicate consisted of ten companies. Its offices were at the Jumeau address of 8 Rue Pastourelle, Paris.

They hoped this grouping

LES BEBES JUMEAU A L'EXPOSITION DE 1900 - HORS CONCOURS

LES BEBES JUMEAU A L'EXPOSITION DE 1900 - HORS CONCOURS

rich blouses and the voluminous chic of their feathered hats, a graceful effect which is achieved by the use of delicate shades of pink and blue." The 1900 Exposition marked the end of the Jumeau era.

These cards are sought after by doll collectors and exposition collectors. Whenever a postcard is not only rare but cross collected, the value increases.

The Encyclopedia of Antique Postcards

EXPOSITION

The Panama Pacific International Exposition (PPIE) was held in San Francisco. The fair was divided into three sections; the *Court of Abundance*, the *Court of Four Seasons* and the *Court of Sun and Stars*.

There were over 100,000 exhibits making the exposition very successful with a profit of over two million dollars. There was a model of the Panama

Canal and a re-creation of the Grand Canyon!

Postcards were a part of the PPIE from the beginning. The supporters of the fair established a statewide California Post Card Week from October 10-17, 1910. The official postcard message was "Get your congressman to Vote for the Panama Pacific International Exposition at the Exposition City, San Francisco, 1915. California Guarantees an Exposition that will be a credit to the Nation." This card is very common and features a girl, a miner and a bear. Supporters mailed nearly 7 million cards that week from California!

Edward Mitchell issued this set of PPIE cards in 1911, numbered 1915 (A-I). Three cards in this set are in sepia, featuring the men involved with the fair; Taft, for ground breaking; Moore, President of the PPIE; and Rolph, the Mayor of San Francisco.

Other PPIE sets were published by Elkus, Weidner, Detroit, Phostint, Tammen, Union Pacific, Behrendt, and Cardinell Vincent, who was the official vendor of cards. Curt Teich of Chicago printed Cardinell Vincent's cards. More than two dozen publishers were involved in producing postcards for this event.

The Denmark building issued the other illustrated set. Rich gold ink accents the fine lithography, making this a very desirable set. §

"Oh! Felix, what a difference just a word from you would make!"

"I'm surprised at you Felix!"

"The Doctor told me to keep this pill on my stomach, but it keeps rolling off!"

Starting with the silent film era, animated cartoons carried audiences through two World Wars, Prohibition, and the Great Depression. One of the best animated silent film stars was Felix the Cat.

Felix was a hero of the common man. Unlike many other cartoon characters, Felix projected his sense of alienation, his hopelessness in not conforming and his constant fight against the elements of hunger and loneliness. He felt rejected by his master every time he was kicked out into the cold and was continually rejected by his lady love, Phyllis.

Yet, he convinced the audience that if you carefully think out your problems, a solution is possible. Unlike Pluto, who carefully thought out every action and then made the wrong choice, Felix folded his hands behind his back and paced out

a correct decision. This pacing was his trademark.

Otto Messmer, working for Pat Sullivan, wrote and animated the first Felix cartoons. The name Felix is attributed to the Paramount producer, John King. Just as Ubbe Iwerks received very little recognition for his creation of Mickey Mouse for Walt Disney, Sullivan's name is most often connected with Felix, though Messmer did the actual drawings.

In 1919, Felix the Cat was very angular and doglike in stance. Many early animated cartoon characters were drawn in solid black to eliminate excessive outlining and make animation easier. Felix was no exception.

After 1921, Sullivan left Paramount and signed a contract with Margaret Winkler, a New York film distributor.

Winkler began worldwide distribution of Felix with a one-reel subject, *Felix Saves The Day*, which appeared in 1922.

With the popularity of the films, it was only natural Felix should join the funny pages. In 1923, Pat Sullivan signed a contract with King Features Syndicate to adapt Felix the Cat to a comic strip. Felix first appeared on August 14, 1923 as a Sunday page.

It was not until four years later, May 9, 1927, that Felix became a daily strip. The strips continued to be signed *Sullivan* after his death, because the copyright passed to his nephew, also named Pat Sullivan.

Sullivan produced over 100 animated Felix cartoons before his death in 1933. Messmer continued to draw Felix as a cartoon character for King Features Syndicate and the New York *Journal American* until

104

"I won't be home 'till morning!"

May EASTER show you the paths of Happiness
"KEEP ON WALKING!"

1951. Messmer continued in animated advertising work until the 1970s. He died in 1983 at the age of 91.

Felix became as popular in England as in the United States. Inter-Art Publishing Company and Woolstone Brothers, both of London, produced postcards featuring Felix the Cat. While these two publishers produced the largest variety of postcards, Bamforth and Company of London and New York also published a few cards.

While inexpensive, compared to other types of comic character merchandise, the postcards reflect the distinctive personality that made Felix the greatest animated film star of the silent era.

Felix did not survive the end of the silent film era. Sullivan did not have the foresight to invest the time or money required to bring Felix into the sound era. Therefore, Felix was obsolete within a year. In 1935, Felix enjoyed a brief revival by through the Van Beuren studio, but it was not successful. Felix was doomed to remain only on the comic pages. §

"Felix, don't you think the best part of the day is the night?"

"I love me! I love me! I'm wild about myself!"

"I don't care nothing for nobody!"

FISHER

This set by Fisher, published by Reinthal and Newman of New York, is numbered RN 186-191, and copyrighted by Charles Scribner and Sons of New York. Each card is signed and titled. These designs were, also, marketed in a long panel frame with a custom designed mat. These panels were the feature of many a Victorian parlor or bedroom.

Harrison Fisher was born July 27, 1875 in Brooklyn, New York, and died in 1934. At age six, Fisher's family moved to Alameda, California, because of his poor health. He attended the San Francisco Art Association and the Mark Hopkins Institute of Art.

Fisher was a major influence on the illustration world, receiving an income of $60,000 in 1910 when $5,000 could purchase a large home. Harrison Fisher's depiction of the Ameri-

The Trousseau

The Proposal

The Wedding

The Honeymoon

First Evening in Their Own Home

Their New Love

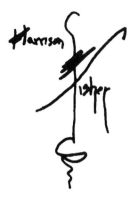

can Girl made his name well known to all magazine readers after 1900. Fisher filled the gap left when Charles Dana Gibson retired in 1905.

Fisher worked for Reinthal and Newman, creating over

200 card designs from 1908 to 1920. One of these cards, *The Kiss,* was described as the best selling postcard ever produced.

Fisher worked mainly for the Detroit Publishing Co. and Reinthal & Newman. The hardest cards to find are those published by European firms. The true rarities of Fisher's are those cards created in small numbers featuring advertising

messages, especially those that relate to his illustrated novels.

This card is a double fold postcard advertising *Nedra*, a novel which Fisher illustrated. Printed by the publisher in a casual handwritten message style are the words, "Nedra Island, Sept. 16, 1905... This is the most fascinating spot on earth. If you cannot join us,

you can at least read all about it in Mr. McCutcheon's new book. Ever yours, Tennys." On the inside is the printed message, "Dear Sirs, Please send me from your first supply ...... copies of NEDRA, The New Novel by GEORGE BARR McCUTCHEON, Author of *Beverly of Graustark*, Yours truly," §

FLOWER CHILDREN

This Nash set, G-53, comes with and without months of the year captions. The G stands for greetings. Flowers were always popular but illustrated books and lavish gardens were only for the rich. With the industrial revolution, flowers came within reach of the common man. Today, most floral cards are inexpensive, because of the large supply. §

January - Geranium

February - Snowdrop

March - Crocus

April - Jonquil

May - Apple Blossom

June - Rose

July - Poppy

August - Hollyhock

September - Golden Rod

October - Cosmos

November - Aster

December - Holly

Jason Frexias worked for the John Winsch Publishing Company of New York. While Samuel L. Schmucker created the lovely girls, Jason Frexias created the wonderful round baby faced children with starfish hands.

He created many Easter, Valentine, St. Patrick's Day and Halloween postcard designs for Winsch. These designs are shown here to illustrate how publishers would take advantage of artists that did not copyright their illustrations.

Frexias was commissioned to design a Halloween series. Later, the publisher lifted the child and placed her atop an egg and then atop a heart to create two more holiday postcards to sell. Frexias was not paid for these.

One Valentine figure was lifted so poorly that the child still held the lid to a jack-o-lantern in her hand while the center motif was a flaming heart for Valentine's Day.

The lifted designs can usually be identified by a lack of detail in the background and illustrations not in the keeping with the artist's style. This is evident when European publishers pirated his John Winsch postcard designs. §

Circa 1914

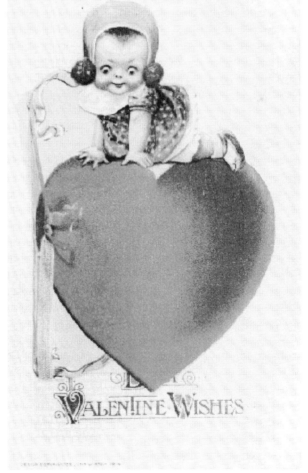

Commissioned in 1905 by Frog in the Throat Lozenge Company, this twelve card set is very elusive. The cards in this set are oversized, 4 by 5¾ inches. Because of this design idiosyncrasy, Victorian collectors severly trimmed most of the cards to fit into standard collecting albums of the period.

The script titles, printed on the cards by the publisher, suggest many of the same advertising ploys engaged in by today's advertisers. *A Social Success* indicates these were accepted by everyone who was anyone. Yet, they were *Pleasant to take* and *Fore Everybody*. The company bragged that Frog in the Throat was *A universal favorite*, that there was *Nothing better*, and that they were the *A Favorite at all times* and *Popular Everywhere*.

My old friend, Dr. Frog even recommends them *For Singers*. This *Innocent and Instantaneous* lozenge *Don't be without it*. The company even suggested that Dr. Frog was so popular he, *Needs no introduction*.

The women are dressed in fancy clothes and intriguing hats. The colors used are powder blue, deep red, green and black. Furs, big bows and

110

plumes are prevalent. The women are both blondes and brunettes.

This 12 card set has an undivided back with the imprint, *Private Mailing Card*, which means only the address was allowed on the back. It was not until 1907 in the United States that a message could be added to the address side. The copyright date is 1905 and, while the artist is unidentified, the illustrated women look very much like the work of Grace Weiderseim-Drayton's magazine cover art of that period.

A similar set of Frog in the Throat cards was issued in the standard 2¾ by 4¾ inch size. There are ten cards in this set with the following titles: *Drives Away Cold Demons, Everybody's Taking Them, Fine For Smoker's Throat, Follow the Leader, For Dry Husky Throats, For Public Speakers, For That Tickling Sensation, Good In Stormy Weather, Renews the Voice for Singers,* and *Stop Your Coughing.*

Regardless of which set you collect, a set of these cards is hard to complete. Many cards have cross collecting interests, such as the card with a camera and the one with a golfing motif. If you are missing these, they may be filed in those categories, or even under frogs because the advertising message is subtle and the company by-line small. §

GASSAWAY

Katharine Gassaway designed postcards for Raphael Tuck, National Art, Rotograph and Ullman Manufacturing Company from 1906 to 1909. Much of Gassaway's work for Tuck is unsigned, but her distinctive style is easily recognized. A wonderful series she did for Tuck is number 501, *Crimson and Gold.*

Her children have big expressive eyes and very round faces. The style is bold and simple with plain backgrounds. One Rotograph set, featuring children of many nations, is highly collected, but most collectors underrate much of her other work.

Her signature is as stylized as her work, with carefully printed letters spelling *Katharine Gassaway* surrounded by a rounded corner box. Two sets are illustrated here to encourage new collectors to take a good look at her work while it is still very reasonable.

Her work is as good in quality as Drayton, Clapsaddle or O'Neill, but at a fraction of the cost. §

Katharine Gassaway

Rotograph
Company
of
New York
F.L. 117-121
& F.L. 132

1 Year

2 Years

3 Years

4 Years

5 Years

6 Years

GOLLIWOGGS

The Golliwogg was to Great Britain's boys and girls what the Kewpie was to American children. Both characters started as illustrations and gradually expanded into the markets of dolls, pottery and jewelry.

The Golliwogg was the creation of artist Florence Kate Upton. Golly first appeared in 1895 in *Adventures of Two Dutch Dolls and a Golliwogg*. This was the first of a series of thirteen books. Florence Upton produced the drawings while her sister created the verse.

Unfortunately for the Uptons, they did not copyright the Golliwogg character. It became so popular that many postcard artists found a way of incorporating the image into their work. Attwell, Studdy, Kennedy, and Lewin designed Golliwogg cards. The signed Upton postcards were taken from the pages of her thirteen books.

A copycat artist designed the illustrated postcard set, not Florence Upton. Yet, the large images, subtle color and silver backgrounds make these postcards very collectible. §

Silver Backgrounds

GREINER

Magnus Greiner designed series 791, published by the International Art Company. Collectors have named the set: *The Adventures of Molly and Teddy*. Collectors, not the publisher, have assigned the titles of each card. This set was created both flat printed and embossed, with and without Christmas greetings.

Greiner did several sets for the International Art Company including Dutch children against a blue tile background. Greiner worked for Tuck creating *Idyls*, *Little Sunbeams*, *Nymphs* and *Golden Cords*.

The *M. Greiner,* in a script signature, is often hidden in the design. Each of these cards is signed, but you must look carefully. §

Molly on the Garden Wall

Molly's Charge

Teddy's Nurse

Teddy's Capture

If Teddy were a Man

Rambles of Molly and Teddy

GRIGGS

Was H.B. Griggs a man or a woman? This question has intrigued card collectors ever since Elisabeth Austin published her checklist over twenty years ago. Speculation has appeared on both sides. But, as Austin said, "Must we know in order to enjoy the artist's skill?"

Black Children Series 2217

Ladies Series 2218

Griggs illustrated cards for New Year's Day, St. Patrick's Day, Thanksgiving, Valentine's Day, Easter, Christmas, Washington's Birthday, Halloween, and birthdays.

There are over 500 signed Griggs cards and another 200 unsigned. All this work was done for one publisher, Leubrie and Elkus of New York. The cards were printed in Germany. Since few cards are found with the Leubrie and Elkus publishing byline without being the work of Griggs, perhaps all Griggs work was self-published or Griggs was related to Leubrie or Elkus. More likely, the publishers knew they had a good thing in Griggs and put Griggs under exclusive contract. As collectible and appealing as they are today, they must have been equally appealing during the postcard era. With the beginning of the war, many publishers including L & E lost their businesses, because all their production work was done in Germany.

The cards begin as early as 1907, and these are rare. The *Votes For Women* Washington card is the most sought after of Griggs' postcards. This card doesn't give us a clue about Griggs position because there are two messages. One half of the card says, *Votes for Women*. The other half is delivered by George Washington saying, *Did I Save my Country for This!* This middle of the road position might suggest H.B.G. was

Cupids Series 2219

White Children Series 2220

a man. Yet, Clapsaddle designed cards on both sides of the issue. This usually was a man's point of view; women either had no comment, or were strongly pro-suffrage.

Only two cards carry full signatures, *H.B. Griggs*. Both are in the number 2233 Thanksgiving Day series. §

GROUND HOG DAY

Punxsutawney, Pennsylvania, is the center of the folklore for Ground Hog Day. In the early 1880s, a group of bored men went to the woods, dug up several woodchucks, and roasted them. This meal, followed by large quantities of white lightning, became a yearly tradition on February 2nd.

Before dinner, club members dress to the "nines," gather at a small park, known as Goddlers Knob, where the president of the club taps on the bunker door. The woodchuck named, Punxsutawney Phil appears.

If he sees his shadow, he hides for six more weeks of winter. This tale is more fiction than fact, because the early cards seem to indicate, on sunny days, the ground Hog comes out to play.

The Henderson Lithographic Company issued this Comic Series 101. §

Henderson
Lithographic Company
of Cincinnati

S
E
R
I
E
S

1
0
1

GUTMANN

Bessie Collins Pease was born in Philadelphia, April 8, 1876. She had formal art training from 1893 until 1901, at the Philadelphia School of Design for Women, The Chase School of Art and The Art Student's League of New York.

In 1903, while in New York, she went to work for Gutmann and Gutmann, Inc., an art publishing business. On July 14, 1906, at the age of thirty, she married Hellmuth Gutmann. They had three children, Alice, Lucille and John. Many illustrations featuring

lished work was for *St. Nicholas Magazine* illustrating poems for F.S. Gardiner's *On the Hillside* and Clara Odell Lyon's *Brave Annabel Lou*.

She spent most of her childhood in Mount Holly, New Jersey. Her art studios were at her homes in South Orange and Island Heights. Her forty year career produced over 600 published works. She quit illustration work in 1947 because of failing eyesight. Her husband died on April 26, 1948. She died, on September 29, 1960. Bessie Pease Gutmann is bur-

ing Women (501-504), Young Girls (800-804), Babies (901-904), Mothers with Babies (1000-1004), Young Women (1100-1104), The Five Senses (1200-1204) and The Events in a Woman's Life (1300-1304), according to Dr. Victor Christie.

In 1909, Gutmann did twelve illustrations, numbered 120-131, for advertising postcards published by Brown and Bigelow Company as individual calendar pages with a hole in the top. They were designed to be sent to customers and were

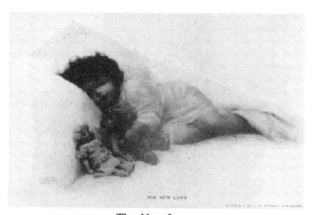

The New Love

Foster Mother

children, were of her children.

Gutmann was an accomplished artist in oil, watercolor, charcoal and pastels, the later being her choice of media. She produced a great variety of prints, calendars, postcards and book illustrations. Her most famous works were two prints, *A Little Bit of Heaven*, modeled after her daughter, Lucille, and *Awakening*. She did illustrated advertisements for Gutmann and Gutmann. Her earliest pub-

ied in Mt. Holly, New Jersey.

The sixty five known postcards of Bessie Pease Gutmann are highly collected and a challenge to find. They were produced from 1909 to 1913, with most of the work done in 1911. The first cards were printed in Germany, but after the high import tariff act of 1909, they were mainly published by the New York firm, Reinthal and Newman.

Her postcards were published in five card sets featur-

used from 1909 to 1911. She did two other advertising cards using her postcard images, *Virginia* and *Strenuous*. §

The First Born

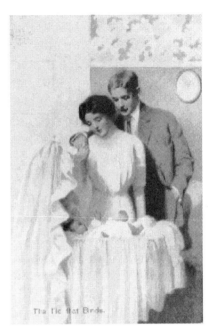

Bessie Pease Gutmann

The Tie that Binds

Bessie Pease Gutmann

Delighted

Bessie Pease Gutmann

Love is Blind

HALLOWEEN

The postcards, published by John Winsch, are among the most desirable of American holiday cards. The best within this group are those for Halloween.

Several appear in sets of six but most are sets of four. All are highly collected. The six card set featured here has designs that are easier to find, while not inexpensive. The three card group is among the rarest of already hard to find cards. To date, collectors have seen only three cards of the set.

While the center motif images appear on other Winsch sets, the deep purple borders make these very unusual. Samuel L. Schmucker created many of the Winsch Halloween cards, most having very bright colors with beautiful women.

Winsch crafted his postcards well with heavy rich ink and embossing. The Schmucker designs were created in America, but sent to Germany for printing. Some have booklets attached, while others have die cuts that project out from the background of the card.

The John Winsch Halloween postcards were published from 1911 to 1915. §

HALLOWEEN

On Halloween, Stick two lit candles in a pumpkin, twirl it around and if they go out everything is OK but beware if they stay lit, you'll be - but say girlie, if that chap with you can't even put a candle out - tie a can to him - quick.

On Halloween, when the moon goes behind the cloud, grinning cats kiss girls on the lips. Only one remedy: keep them covered - but no doubt your friend will attend to that.

On Halloween, take the seeds from a Pumpkin, place them in front of the sofa in the form of a cross -- then the Witches won't bother you that's a hard name to call ma and pa but they were young themselves once and won't mind it.

On Halloween, Goblins have been known to fly away with Fair Maidens. Therefore 'tis best to have some one hold you and tightly too, -- because Goblins are strong.

On Halloween, throw an Apple Peeling over your shoulder and if it spells kiss go to it. It's bound to work, girls, Any old thing looks like kiss to the right fellow if the time, place and the girl are there.

On Halloween, take a candle, look into a mirror, then over your shoulder you'll see your future hubby's face... In the excitement the candle goes out... this affair must be prearranged to be successful...

HAYS

Margaret Gebbie Hays was an artist who never escaped the shadow of her younger sister, Grace Gebbie Weiderseim - Drayton. Hays was born July 31, 1874 in Philadelphia. George Gebbie, her father, was a successful art publisher.

The Gebbie children were educated at home, and then at the convent of Notre Dame of Philadelphia. At age 19, Margaret married Frank Allison Hays. She died in 1925.

As Grace Drayton's talent developed, Margaret spent her time producing the verse for Grace's many works. They collaborated on *Mother Goose Rhymes* which ran five years in *Associated Sunday Magazine*.

One of Hays' sets was pub-lished by Nister and distributed by E.P. Dutton of New York. Series numbers 2748-2753 feature Miss Polly Pig-tail sending Valentine greetings. §

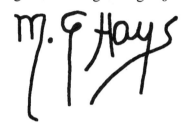

HOLD TO LIGHT

Any postcard that can be held to the light resulting in a changed image can rightly be called a Hold to Light. Postcard collectors break this category into two distinctive types of cards.

The first, die cut Hold to Lights, use a process where several layers of paper are molded together. The top layer has small die cut shapes or holes punched through that surface only. When held to the light these die cut windows shine with the illuminated color of the thinner papers below.

The second type of Hold to Lights is called transparencies. This type of card is not as thick or ridged as the die cuts. There are several layers of very thin paper bonded together to form the postcard. The hidden inner layers contain an additional image seen only after the card is held to a light.

The cheapest type of transparency when held to the light produces a simple line drawing in black of an additional figure, such as a Santa Claus coming down the chimney. These were usually produced in America and are the most common.

Meteor published the next most common transparency. These feature more intricate images. The least collected of this publisher has very little action to the design. For example, the outer image is of a mountain. When held to the light, a moon, stars, or lightning appears. While these are

colorful and fun to see the first time, there are Meteor transparencies that have much more action.

For example, the best show conversions of Winter scenes to Summer scenes. The wintry scene of a horse drawn sleigh when held to the light becomes two children riding in a goat cart on a Summer's day. Everything changes, the scene, the costumes, the colors, and the mood. These are the best of the Meteors.

Cosmos published the harder to find transparencies. These transparencies usually are passed over because they look like thin paper postcards with images in a dull olive green monotone. Yet, when held to the light, a finely detailed full color image appears to delight any collector. All types of Hold to Lights require a strong light to enjoy the full effect.

Joseph Koehler published some of the finest die cut Hold to Light American views. The complete set of Koehler Hold to Lights has 113 cards featuring views of New York, Coney Island, Philadelphia, Boston, Niagara Falls, the Hudson River, Atlantic City, Buffalo, Washington, D.C., and Chicago.

The cards are done in vibrant colors with cut out windows of red, yellow and blue. The identical views were published without the Hold to Light feature. The rarest of Koehler Hold to Lights is the card, *Fight-*

ing the Flames from the Coney Island postcard set. The Uncle Sam Santas are the rarest of Hold to Lights. §

Art Nouveau Hold to Lights

U N C L E   S A M   S A N T A S

ICART

Louis Justin Icart was the first son of Jean and Elisabeth Icart, born September 12, 1888 in Toulouse, France. Early on he was called by his initials, *L.I.*, pronounced el-e. He even signed his art work *Helli*.

Helli attended a private Catholic school and was a good student. He participated in school plays and fell in love with the work of Victor Hugo. His father wanted him to be-

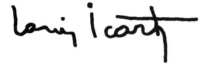

come a banker but Helli was most interested in the arts. He really wanted to be an actor.

Icart, after graduation and mandatory military service, went to Paris looking for a job. To earn living expenses he worked for a small postcard publisher hand-tinting the work of other postcard artists. Like

many small publishers in Paris, they specialized in actresses for export. This type of semi-risque card was very popular.

This exposed Icart to the subject matter that was to eventually become his trademark. He learned art techniques, like etching and aquatint. Some cards even taught Helli about lithography and photo repro-

duction. This experience may have taken years to learn at an art college, but within months he was creating hundreds of designs all signed Helli. These were done from 1907 to 1908.

There are only eight known cards signed Icart. Seven cards are from series number 48 by Marque of Paris, titled *L'Eternal Feminin Sanquines*,

featuring women on a peach background. The other card featuring a woman and a dog is number 1785 by Galerie Lutelia of Paris but printed in Italy. These are easier

to find, but, as a rule, command a higher price. Perhaps collectors are unfamiliar with the Helli signature.

Early in 1914, Icart met Fanny Volmers, who became his model and lover for over 35

years. By that spring, Icart had left his wife to live with Volmers. They never married as his wife, a devote Catholic, refused to divorce him. Volmers and Icart had one child, a daughter named Reine, meaning queen. Icart had a long and industrious career ending with his death on December 30, 1950 at his home in France. §

The city of Sleepy Eye, Minnesota, was named for an Indian chief, *Old Sleepy Eye*, of the Lower Sissenton Sioux tribe. In 1824, the tribe sent him to Washington, D.C., where President Monroe gave him the title *Chief*. Sleepy Eye was not known for his abilities as a warrior, or even as a great hunter, but as a friend to the white man.

Sleepy Eye, Minnesota, became a town in 1872, after

the Chicago and Northwestern Railroad was established. The Sleepy Eye Mill followed in 1883 and became one of the leading producers of flour in the world. The Sleepy Eye trademark became a symbol of quality for the flour that won the Grand Prize at the 1904 St. Louis World's Fair.

This nine card set was available as a premium from the flour mill for ten cents. The most desirable postcard in the group is the Old Sleepy Eye Indian trademark. The monument is least desirable. §

Franz Huld

ENVELOPE

SINGLE CARD

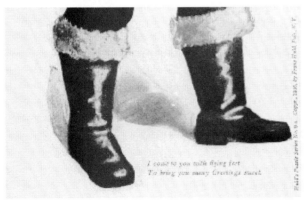

INSTALLMENTS

Postcard publishers were always seeking ways to increase their sales. With installment cards, customers were forced to purchase 3 or more cards.

Installment cards were very

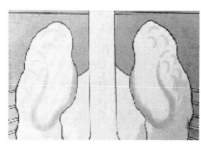

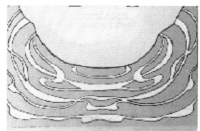

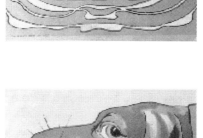

popular both here and abroad. European collectors call them puzzle cards. The puzzle was to figure out what the final picture was going to be upon receiving one of these cards each day by mail. It is amazing that these cards are often postally

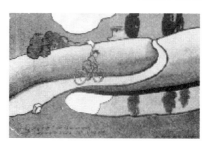

used on consecutive days.

This type of novelty postcard was the easiest for publishers to make and scores of sets have been documented. The large 12-24 card sets often feature a central figure, like Napoleon, Joan of Arc, Czar Nicholas, Franz Joseph or Sarah Bernhardt, with each individual card depicting part of the personalitie's life.

Often, each individual card gives no clear idea that it is part of an installment group. For example, when examining the four card Santa head, the top two cards would give you a good clue with the Santa's eye on the individual card. However, the bottom two cards could be very easily filed with Christmas children cards, as they give very

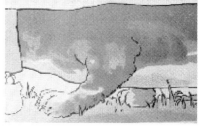

132

INSTALLMENTS

little clue that they are a part of an installment set. The challenge is always to find missing cards in an installment set, but it can be done. Only three of the four cards in the installment Santa head were found at one time, the other card was finally reunited with its companions after fifteen years of searching.

Installment sets were published by Rose Company, Wildwood Post Card Company, Walter Wirth, Rotograph, Walter Wellman and many European firms.

Franz Huld published the most desirable American installment cards from 1905-1907. Huld titled his cards, *puzzle cards,* which sold, with an envelope depicting the final picture, for a dime. §

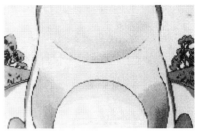

 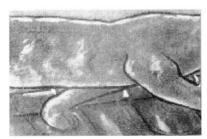 

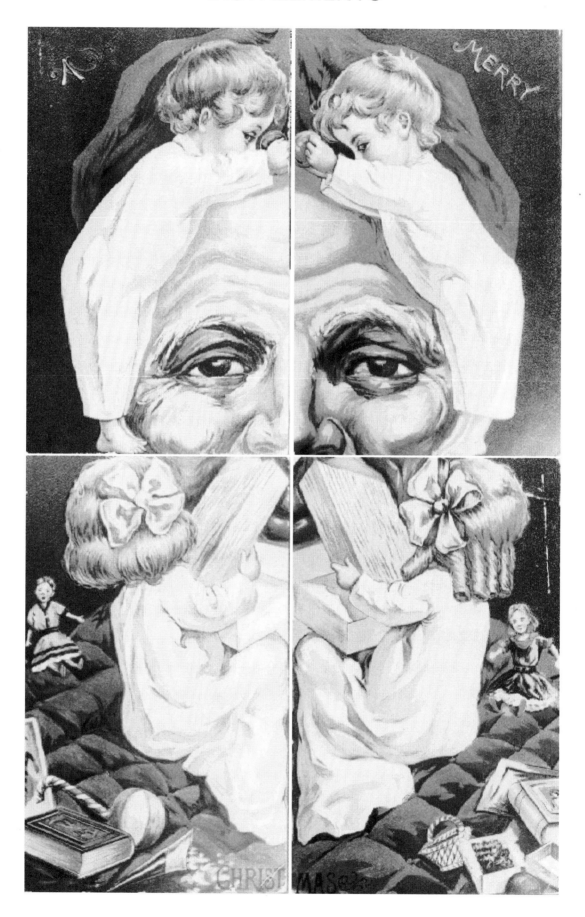

Sweets to the Sweet

Kick out the Grouch

Cultivate Repose

During the same time the Kewpie doll was bombarding the world, Kate Jordan created the small all-bisque creature called a Happifat. Patented in 1914, the Butler Brothers Company sold them at $2.25 for an assorted dozen, or a four inch pair for 30 cents.

The Happifats were surely named for their big smiles and equally big tummies. As appealing as they are to postcard collectors, they have a hair style only a mother could love, with one large curl in front and two swags of hair on the back

of an otherwise bald head.

Besides the dolls, Kate Jordan designed a signed set of six postcards published by the Edward Gross Company. They have the same dull olive green background as the Gross Publishing Company's O'Neill Kewpies. The six cards are individually numbered. §

Turn your Back on Care

Gather Ye Rosebuds while Ye may

To bring You Luck

Postcard collectors best know Hamilton King as the creator of the Coca-Cola girl. This rare advertising card exhibits the quality and style of King's work.

If this card is elusive or beyond your budget, consider his other postcard work. The designs of full figured women are great, but the portrait heads are nearly identical to the Coke girl, at only a fraction of the cost.

The Coca-Cola Company copyrighted the painting, used for this Coke postcard, in 1909. Wolf and Company of Philadelphia, Pennsylvania, published the postcard. The card is nearly devoid of color except for the red border, red Coca-Cola logo, and a red flower; yet, it will mesmerize the viewer and card collector.

THE COCA-COLA GIRL

DRINK DELICIOUS Coca-Cola

The only other Coca-Cola advertising postcard features a girl in an automobile, referred to in the past as the *Duster Girl*. Yet, Petretti's *Coca-Cola Collectibles Guide* corrects this title to *Motor Girl* through other documentation.

King did covers for *Theatre Magazine* and sheet music for Ziegfield Follies. §

Hamilton King

Raphael Kirchner was born in Vienna, Austria, in 1876. He attended the Akademie der bildenden Kunste in Vienna. He earned a living as a book illustrator and painter of portraits of women from high society in Vienna.

Kirchner settled in Paris, France, at the turn of the century and stayed in France until the beginning of World War I when he moved to the United States. He died in New York, August 2, 1917.

His work could be classified as a forerunner to pin-up girls. His illustrations are very provocative. He worked for several French magazines; *La Vie Parisienne*, *L'Assiette au Beurre*, and *Sketch*.

His first postcard work was in 1898 with designs for Philipp and Kramer. Kirchner's postcards number over 1,000 designs, yet are not commonly found in America.

His postcard success can be measured by his *Geisha* series. It successfully reprinted four times for a total of 40,000 copies.

Kirchner's work appeared in many other forms. An American publisher, The House of Art in New York did a series of prints, approximately 11 by 14 inches, of Kirchner's work. Some titles are *Between the Acts*, *The Fox*, and *Mystery*. They did a series of ten titled: *Envy, Gluttony, Covetousness, Expiation, Luxury, Pride, An-*ger, *Sloth, Temptation*, and *Dream*. These ten original designs hung in the foyer of the Century Theatre, in New York City.

These came in monotone and hand colored versions. Many of these designs first appeared as postcards; called *The Seven Deadly Sins*, the French title, *Les Peches Capitaux* published by Marque L-E of Paris. The French set is unclothed, while the later New York series is clothed in costumes designed for the Ziegfeld Follies. Reinthal and Newman of New York published this series of ten as postcards.

Some of Kirchner's early postcard images appear on 6 by 15 inch silk panels. These de-

SANTOY I-VI

signs are from his early period. The colors are very delicate and appealing. This type of material is rare and often damaged, when found. Deteriorating silk appears to melt and is identified by very fine lines of missing threads. When this has happened, professional restoration is needed immediately. Besides prints, Kirchner illustrated several books. Two are *Le Mal de Paris* and *L'Apbrodite Modern*, circa 1913. Examples of his work can be found on sheet music and wine labels.

The postcards designs of Raphael Kirchner can be divided into three periods. The late period, the newest postcards, is identified by the publisher's name on the front of the card, usually Bruton Galleries or Alpha. The middle period always has the title of the individual postcard printed in French on the back. The early period is everything else and usually is distinguished by the strong art nouveau style, chromo lithographic printing, and undivided backs.

Kirchner worked for many different publishers, including Raphael Tuck, Theo. Stroefer, M.M. Wien, Brother Kohn, and Philipp & Kramer. While most of Kirchner's work is elusive, the rarest is his Santa Claus image and the die cut Hold to Lights. Kirchner's women were mystical creatures of perfume, cigarettes, opium and eroticism. §

RAPHAËL KIRCHNER.

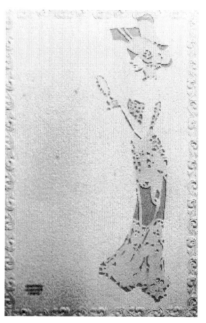

Alphabet Series

KLEIN

Catherine Klein was born in 1861 and died in 1929. She created some of the most sought after floral designs. Raphael Tuck & Sons, International Art Company, Theo. Stroeffer, and Meissner & Buch published her work. Klein created over 2000 still life portraits featuring fruits, vegetables and nuts.

The Klein alphabet series 148, featured here, is the most desirable of her postcard work. While the alphabet design seems to pop off the page in black and white, the subtle use of color makes these cards sometimes hard to distinguish from her regular floral work. The letters U-V-W-X-Y-Z are the hardest to find.

The cards are most often collected by china painters to help them understand the subtle use of shading, which was her forte. Besides postcards, she created book illustrations and yard long pictures. Modern greeting card companies have reprinted her work. §

Melanie (Mela) Koehler-Broman was born in 1885. She was a graphic designer and illustrator. Her major publishers were Brother Kohn Wien (BKWI), Munk, and the Wiener Werkstaette (WW). She did nearly 150 designs for the Wiener Werkstaette alone. She died in 1960. §

Brother Kohn Wien I (BKWI)

KRUSE

Mother's Darling

Out for an airing

Published by Raphael Tuck, series 8677, *Quaint Little Folk*, feature the dolls of Kathe Kruse.

In a 1912 *Ladies' Home Journal* story, Kruse wrote, "It happened thus: My husband did not wish to buy any dolls for our children. He disliked extremely the stiff, cold, breakable dolls." What is a mother to do? Her two daughters Maria and Sophia, "stood with eyes full of expectation before me and wanted a doll."

Käthe Kruse

Going to Market

Left in charge

She fashioned the first doll for the children from a potato wrapped in a towel. The sand body nestled in their arms and "the little head fell to the side and always demanded to be thought of and to be protected."

After exhibiting her homemade dolls in a 1910 Christmas exhibition at the Berlin department store of Hermann Tietz, "The triumphal march began, and neither the dolls nor I know how it happened, for they were thought out only for my own children, were made only for them," said Kruse. §

Family Cares

Allow me to introduce you

Labor conquers everything

Service shall with steeled sinews toil

Labor Day was declared a national holiday in 1894 and is observed on the first Monday in September. It was to honor the work ethic and unify the labor movement. It has become a symbol of summers end. There are two sets of Labor Day cards, one by Nash, the other by Lounsbury.

Nash Publishing Company produced this set commemorating Labor Day. The two card set is a well designed and colorful pair. One card features Miss Liberty with two laborers in front of an American eagle.

The caption reads, *Service shall with steeled sinews toil, and labour will refresh itself with hope*. The other card says, *Labor conquers everything— the strictest law oft becomes the severest injustice*. This card features a single workman holding a flag with the eagle and shield in the background.

According to *Picture Postcards in the United States 1893-1918*, Hubin's, on the Boardwalk in Atlantic City, may have been the sole distributor of these cards. Hubin's sold them for many years during the postcard

craze. These are desirable but not rare.

The other set, designed by Lounsbury Publishing, has four cards and are much harder to find. Some consider these the best of American holiday postcards. They are titled, *Makers of Prosperity*, *The Man in Overalls*, *Labor Taking a Day off*, and *Our Latest Holiday*.

Of this group, the last card is most sought after because it features a parade with Labor Day, followed by Thanksgiving, Santa Claus, New Years, Washington and Uncle Sam. §

LE MAIR

Henriette Willebeek le Mair was born in Rotterdam, Holland, in 1889 to a wealthy family. Many nursery scenes depicted on her postcards are similar to the surroundings in which she lived.

At the age of fifteen, she had her first book published in France, *Premieres Rondes Enfantines*. When she was twenty she conducted a school in her home for small children. It was here that she observed the carefree spirit of children's make believe. Her postcard work reflected the style and grace of these children.

In 1911, Augener Limited commissioned her to do a series of books with rhymes set to music. These books, *Our Old Nursery Rhymes*, *Little Songs of Long Ago*, *Little People*, *The Childrens Corner*, *Schumanns Album of Children's Pieces* and *Old Dutch Nursery Rhymes* were published from 1911 to 1917. During this time, eleven series, of twelve postcards each, published by Augener, were taken from these books. The postcard sets can be confusing because these cards were interchanged when the sets were issued and reissued until the late 1930s.

In 1920, Le Mair married Baron van Tuyll van Serooskerken. After that she produced very little work, instead turning her energies to helping her husband in his role as National Representative to the Sufi movement.

She did a book each year for 1925, 1926, and 1939. A book of *Christmas Carols for Young Children* was published for the first time in 1976, ten years after her death.

In 1925, she designed advertisements for the Colgate Company, used as color plates for that year's book. §

LEWIN

Frederick George Lewin was born in Bristol, England, in 1861, the son of a sea captain. His interest in journalism caused him to take a position as a reporter, at the age of twenty, with the *Western Daily Press*.

He was a self-taught artist who worked for *Punch* magazine and several newspapers, such as, *Zig Zag*, *Magpie*, and the *Bristol Guardian*. For nearly fifty years, the *Bristol Times and Mirror* featured his drawings.

He illustrated and wrote, *ABC Book for Good Boys and Girls* and *Rhymes of Ye Olde Sign Boards* in 1911. The next year, he illustrated *Characters from Dickens* by R.W. Matz. He did not do another book until 1922, when he illustrated Arthur Salmon's, *Bristol City Suburbs*

After a long history of heart ailments, he died on October 14, 1933 in his home in Bristol, England. §

Best Wishes for An Enjoyable X'mas.
J. Salmon # 3064

and Countryside.

E.W. Savory published Lewin's earliest postcards in 1905 and 1906. Later, J. Salmon and Inter-Art published the majority of his cards. He did work for Munk, Pulman, Birn Brothers, Woolstone Brothers, and Bamforth. During his career, he produced nearly 500 designs, nearly half published by J. Salmon. The work published by the small firm of E.W. Savory is the hardest to find.

He signed his cards with both full signature and just F.G.L. His subject matter is usually Black children, Dickens' characters or cartoons about World War I.

Lewin spent his entire life in or near Bristol, England.

Two Blacks don't make a white.
J. Salmon # 2513

" Say Honey ! d'you like Black chicken ? "
" 'Deed I do ! "

Honey! d'you like Black chicken?
J. Salmon # 2920

LEYENDECKER

Joseph Christian Leyendecker was born March 23, 1874, in Germany. His brother, Frank Xavier, was born three years later and his sister, Augusta, was born after the family immigrated to Chicago, Illinois, in 1882 when Joseph was eight years old.

Even at that age, he was drawing on every surface. By age 16, he chose art as a full time career. Because of the families' poor financial background, Joseph was unable to attend art school. He apprenticed at J. Manz and Company of Chicago, Illinois. When he completed his apprenticeship, he spent his salary of two dollars a week to attend classes three nights each week at the famous Art Institute.

For five years, he studied under John H. Vanderpoel, who helped him develop his talent as a draftsman. His brother, Frank, took many of the same classes.

When Joseph was 21 and Frank was 18, their parents had saved enough to help send the boys to Paris, France. The two lived together, taking classes and touring the cities galleries and museums. The city must have been a cultural shock after their lives in Chicago. Much of downtown Chicago was covered with stockyards; in contrast, Paris was covered with art nouveau posters by Mucha, Cheret, and Lautrec.

The brothers were enrolled in the Academie Julian, where Joseph was to shine. Many considered him the most talented young man to attend Julian for many years. Several of his works, completed at school, were part of their permanent collection, until they were destroyed during the war.

Even before leaving school, Joseph won the poster contest sponsored by *The Century* magazine in 1896. He created the illustrated covers for a great Chicago based magazine, *The Inland Printer*, for the entire year of 1897, plus a few for the following two years.

The boys returned to Chicago in 1897 and opened a studio where they successfully received many commissions. Joseph had to work hard all his life. He believed, "If you spend more than you make, it will force you to create."

His first magazine cover for *The Saturday Evening Post* was on May 20, 1899. This led to 321 covers in his lifetime. He specialized in holiday issues. The most sought after, are his New Year's Day babies, which appeared annually for forty years.

In 1900, only a couple of years after opening their Chicago studio, Joseph and Frank moved to New York City, where recognition and commissions were greater. By 1905, Joseph landed what was to be his most important commercial art account, with Cluett, Peabody and Company, Inc., the manufacturers of Arrow brand detachable shirt collars.

Over the next twenty five years, the Arrow shirt man became a symbol of men's fashions in America. In one month in the 1920s the Arrow Man received 17,000 pieces of fan mail. The model for the Arrow Man was Joseph Leyendecker's companion of fifty years, Charles Beach.

Leyendecker started work for B. Kuppenheimer & Company and Interwoven Socks in 1908. In 1912, Kellogg's employed him for a series of corn flake advertisements. With these commissions, he could move to a bigger home.

Leyendecker built a 14 room mansion in New Rochelle in 1914, and commuted to New York City. By 1920, he built a studio at his home and gave up his New York City office. In 1924, his brother Frank died a few months after he and his sister left Joseph's house because of a family quarrel.

He designed his last cover for the *Post* in January, 1943. In 1944, he did a series of war bond posters. Joseph C. Leyendecker died of a heart attack at the age of 77, in his home on July 25, 1951.

His postcard work is very limited. The postcards illustrated were taken from his 1918 Chesterfield Cigarette advertisement posters, produced for Ligget and Myers, Inc. The postcards are not signed, but the signed originals are in the Metropolitan Museum of Art, New York. §

1918
Ligget
and
Myers
Chesterfield
Ads
on
Postcards

Gennaio (January)

Febbraio (February)

Aprile (April)

Giugno (June)

Agosto (August)

Ottobre (October)

MAUZAN

One of the most collected art deco artists is Lucien Achille Mauzan. Born in 1883, Mauzan died in France in 1952. He worked for Alfieri & Lacroix, Bertarelli, Chialtone, Maga and other publishers. Mauzan was a painter, illustrator and sculpturer. Most of his postcard work was published in Italy. This set is not an exception. His women are unique, mildly erotic, and romantic.

Mirande and Marino Carnevale-Mauzan wrote a complete book of Mauzan's postcards titled, *Le Cartes Postales L. A. Mauzan.* Mirande worked very closely with Marino Mauzan, the daughter of the artist.

His postcard sets consist of propaganda about the war from 1915-1919, propaganda about Fascism, woman's charms usually with cupids, humorous satire, and advertising. §

Marzo (March)

Maggio (May)

Luglio (July)

Settembre (September)

Novembre (November)

Dicembre (December)

Little Nemo was the small boy that led a generation of comic strip readers to the fantasy world of Slumberland. Winsor Zenic McCay illustrated Nemo, modeling him after his son, Robert.

The strip first appeared October 15, 1905 in the New York *Herald's* Sunday supplement. The format was similar to *The Dreams of a Rarebit Fiend*, which McCay had done as a full color page, expressing the weird world of dreams.

This strip lacked a fixed cast of characters. He based each story on a different character, who fell asleep, after eating too much Welsh rarebit, and experienced nightmares. McCay perfected the nightmare as an art form and went on to create Little Nemo.

Each week Little Nemo would drift off into Slumberland, whose King was Morpheus, and experience many adventures that lasted until he awoke in the last panel. Awake he must, because Slumberland contained all the classic fears children have while dreaming: towering mushrooms, giant mosquitoes, dragons, green kangaroos, plus the fantasy King, Queen, Prince and Princess.

Little Nemo, like *Alice in Wonderland,* is often the brunt of terrible deeds, perpetrated by the fantasy characters, such as Flip, a cigar-smoking leprechaun, and Impy, a quiet, selfish and cruel cannibal.

Little Nemo's goal was to get to Slumberland and meet King Morpheus's daughter, the Princess. From 1905 to 1911, Nemo, Flip, Princess, Impy, Granny, Hag and King Morpheus traveled from the Candy Islands to the Moon in the New York *Herald.*

Raphael Tuck published this set of twelve cards in 1907 from the New York *Herald.* It has wonderful, rich colors of deep green, dark purple, and the bright gold of royalty mixed with red, white and blue. In this set, Nemo, while in Slumberland, meets the Princess and marries.

McCay said he always had his artistic talent. "I never decided to be an artist," wrote McCay. "Simply, I couldn't stop myself from drawing anything and everything. I drew on fences, the school blackboards, old scraps of paper, sides of barns—I just couldn't stop."

His father, not impressed with his son's artistic talent, did everything to discourage him. He sent McCay to business school in Ypsilanti, Michigan, but McCay rarely attended class. He preferred to spend his time drawing pictures of the patrons of Detroit's dime museums, charging them a quarter. The dime museums were a combination of circus, vaudeville and magic acts.

From his failed business studies, McCay went to Chicago, where he designed advertising posters for a circus company. He moved to Cincinnati where he worked for Morton's Dime Museum, creating scenic sideshow posters. He settled in New York in 1903.

Little Nemo was not McCay's first comic strip. He drew *Little Sammy Sneeze, Hungry Henrietta, Dream of the Rarebit Fiend, Dull Care, Poor Jake, The Man from Montclair, A Pilgrim's Progress,* and *It's*

Nice to Be Married, but his best was *Little Nemo*. Within a few years, *Little Nemo* was published in seven languages, made into a Broadway play and reproduced on clothing, toys, cards, and games.

McCay's artistic genius was showcased with his superb creation of *Little Nemo In Slumberland*. McCay showed the public that newspaper comics could reach the level of real art. His drafting techniques detailed palaces and illustrated his imaginative, distorted, surrealistic, mirrored rooms, staircases and cities of the future.

In 1909, McCay became a famous vaudeville house entertainer by sitting on stage and drawing, with lightning speed, his Little Nemo characters. His precision and wit made him a great success. That year, he became interested in animation and predicted "the future successful artist will be one whose pictures move."

By 1910, McCay had assembled and shot 4,000 animated drawings of Little Nemo that were shown in vaudeville theaters with McCay on stage.

This film is in the archives of the Museum of Modern Art. Another interesting feature was *Gertie the Dinosaur*, made in 1911.

His great success brought him the luxury of $200 a week, when the average worker brought home $9 a week. William Randolph Hearst, who was notorious for stealing talent away from his competition by offering outrageous salaries, succeeded in luring McCay from the *Herald* to the *American*. McCay was paid $1,000 a week! This was 1911.

Little Nemo was renamed *In the Land of Wonderful Dreams*, when McCay made the move but the quality of the art and printing deteriorated. Hearst decided McCay was a serious artist who should illustrate Hearst's editorials.

Little Nemo made his last appearance in the *American* on December 12, 1913. McCay stayed at the *American* until the end of his contract in 1924. When he returned to *Little Nemo* and the *Herald*, no one cared.

McCay was a pioneer of American comic art. The popularity of the comic strip created a loyal paying audience, who would buy newspapers just to follow their favorite strips.

This comic art success established that money could be made from the art and the artists became self supporting. Because of McCay's success, others were attracted to the field, which eventually extended beyond newspapers to toys, dolls, games, clothing, jewelry, and animated films.

McCay's work influenced Walt Disney, when doing *Snow White*, *Fantasia*, and the pink-elephant scenes in *Dumbo*.

Winsor Zenic McCay was born in Spring Lake, Michigan, on September 26, 1869. He insisted it was 1871, perhaps to appear younger than 25, when he took a 14 year old bride, Maude. They had two children. McCay died July 26, 1934. §

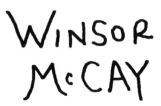

TUCK Series Number 6 © 1907 New York Herald Company

The cartoon strip, *Bringing Up Father,* appeared off and on in the Hearst daily papers from 1913 to 1916 before it became a regular feature. From 1916 until 1918 the strip appeared regularly in the dailies but on April 14, 1918, it made its debut in the Sunday paper. George McManus created and drew the strip until 1954.

He based the strip on a 1893 play by William Gill, *The Rising Generation.* The premise is that Maggie, who took in wash, and Jiggs, who was a mason, win the Irish Sweepstakes and become wealthy.

Maggie wants to move up in society, but Jiggs just wants to go to the local pub for cards and food with his old friends. This conflict of interest is cartooned in a play format, with hilarious conversations. Jiggs is constantly trying to duck out to the tavern and Maggie is constantly throwing a rolling pin or a household item at Jiggs.

Bringing Up Father is one of the few strips where the social classes are mixed in a delightful sequence. At one time or another, the top bosses, the maid and the unemployed are paraded in and out of the strip by McManus.

The envelope for this set of six postcards says, "Don't Throw Away A Laugh, It's Bad Luck. There are six rib ticklers in this package that leads to scores of side splinters."

It was a clever way for the *North American* to get the public to read their advertising message. Each card features

Maggie: My! But this is a dismal day.
Jiggs: Yes, but it will be all to the Merry when the North American comes.

Jiggs: I'm gonna sneak out an git a North American.

Jiggs: Wake me up when the North American comes!

the characters with an advertising plug for the Sunday edition of the *North American*. The Star Company copyrighted this oversized advertising set in 1919.

George McManus was born in St. Louis on January 23, 1884. McManus started cartooning at the age of 16. His first strip was *Alma and Oliver*. In 1904, McManus went to work in New York for Joseph Pulitzer's *World*. There he created, *Snoozer*, *The Merry Marcelene*, *Panhandle Pete*, *Nibsy the Newsboy in Funny Fairyland*, *Cheerful Charley* and *Let George Do It*. The best strip he created for the *World*, was *The Newlyweds*.

In 1912, McManus switched to Hearst's New York *North American*. There he changed the title of *The Newlyweds* to *Their Only Child* and, later, *Baby Snookums*.

On October 22, 1954, George McManus died and Bill Kavanagh wrote the script for *Bringing Up Father*, with Frank Fletcher, illustrating the Sunday strip, and Vernon Green, doing the daily strip. With the death of Green in 1965, Hal Campagna drew the daily strip.

The characters of George McManus' strips are featured on postcards, books, and bisque dolls. They have been adapted to a half dozen screen plays, in some of which, McManus played Jiggs. *Bringing Up Father* was such a loved strip, that on its 25th Anniversary a Congressional dinner was held in Washington, D.C., to celebrate McManus' success. §

Maggie: Isn't this a beautiful Sunday?
Jiggs: It will be when the
North American arrives.

Jiggs: I saw the ad in the North American
so it must be good!

Maggie: Get me a North American
and be quick about it.

Paul Finkenrath of Berlin (PFB) published this postcard set. In addition to the great design and wonderful printing quality, these are mechanical postcards. Red, blue and gold art deco style drapes frame the puppets. Gold stars literally cover the puppeteer's box.

The illustrated set has French titles, but the postcards do appear with English titles. They were also issued as non-mechanical postcards. Once you have seen the action of the mechanical cards, you won't be happy until you own at least one.

Because they are impossible to resist playing with, often the cards are in varying degrees of disrepair. Fre-quently, professional repairs have been made to the delicate legs and sticks. The cards are scarce and should be accepted in less than perfect condition. §

PFB
Series 6012

T U R N   D I A L   A N D   S A N T A   A P P E A R S

"When I'm with you, Mickey, I'm near heaven!"

"Am I making a hit with you?"

"Coo-oo Mickey!"

Walt Disney started the lucrative business of animating figures on film with a collaborator named Ubbe Iwerks. Like all beginners he needed a special figure and found Mickey Mouse, who made his debut in late 1928.

Mickey was an artless, awkward rodent, who squeaked in shrill tones in the early talkies.

Mickey Mouse was a rambunctious, slightly sadistic character. Mickey and Minnie used their fists and twisted animals to produce a chorus of *Turkey in the Straw*, for their screen debut in *Steamboat Willie*.

Shortly after the release of this highly successful film of 1929, postcards were issued in Great Britain, Germany, Holland and France. Many early postcards have captions in both German and English.

The early postcards portray the same sadistic Mickey Mouse. He drank and smoked big cigars, which the modern day Mickey would never dream of doing.

The best postcard material was produced in England, ei-

"Keep your Sunny Side up!"

"I'm not a marrying man!"

"That's what keeps me awake all night!"

"Three Blind Mice!"

"Accept no substitutes!"

"Now, where is that bally cat?"

ther by Inter-Art Company or Valentine & Sons. These cards usually have a snow white background, which is an overlay of white ink on cream paper stock. These cards are hard to find in mint condition.

One of the best Mickey images on postcards, shows him standing in front of a billboard with the names: Dou-

glas Fairbanks, Charlie Chaplin and Mickey Mouse. Mickey has crossed out Fairbanks and Chaplin leaving only his name.

Each Inter-Art Disney postcard is individually numbered, generally with series 7000.

Valentine and Sons, Ltd. started publishing pictorial envelopes in the 1840s. It was not until 1897 that they published

pictorial postcards. The Mickey Mouse 4000 series was published about ten years after his first film. An unused Valentine and Son postcard can be dated by the number in the stamp box. For example, 38-2 indicates a printing in 1938.

Mickey has become the most recognized and celebrated cartoon character in history. §

"We'll be with you soon!"

"-and I'll be there with you when my dreams come true!"

"It may be four years, and it may be for ever!"

The first postcard published featuring the illustrations of Alphonse Maria Mucha was *Le Home Decor*, in 1894. In 1895, Mucha signed a six year contract with Sarah Bernhardt to do her theatrical posters, a turning point in his career.

At this time, a very perceptive printer, Champenois, acquired the exclusive rights to all his productions. Champenois was one of the first, in France, to publish illustrated postcards. From 1898, he systematically reproduced Mucha's most popular designs in seven series of 12 postcards each. He expanded the use of the Mucha images by adapting them to the advertising needs of clients, especially the French department store, Belle Jardiniere.

Champenois' fourth set was the twelve months of the year. This was the most popular of the seven series. He designed the graphic work in 1899 for the covers of 12 issues of the magazine, *Mois Artistique et Litteraire*. It was a great postcard success with several editions printed, including one where the months of the year titles were omitted.

Each card features a woman dressed to protect herself from the climate and surrounded by the vegetation of that month. The postcards were designed for messages to be written on the front and were usually used in this manner.

The chromo lithography, combined with a high quality paper, make these cards very attractive. The design quality is some of Mucha's best with attention paid to the background detail and subtle striking colors. A border of gold ink encircles each design. This is the most often seen set.

The most famous of all postcards is the Mucha designed, *Waverley Cycle*. This, to date, is the world's most expensive postcard. With only a handful of examples known to exist, this 1897 poster was published as a postcard in 1898.

The postcards of Mucha can be divided into two peri-

ods, the French and the Slavic. The postcards, published by Champenois, represent the bulk of the French period. These cards appear with and without advertising.

The Champenois cards are often series of the four seasons, flowers and times of the day, taken from Mucha panels. Many other Champenois postcards appeared as posters, calendars or menus.

The only design created exclusively for a postcard, during the French period, was *A Peasant Woman*, Mucha's contribution to the *Collection des Cent*. This was a set of 100 postcards designed by the top poster artists of the time. Mucha was the only artist to have two postcards to his credit in this set. The other card was *Austro-Hungarian Benevolent Society,* a reworked design.

Mucha moved to America for a time. When he returned he had another turning point in his career. This time he embarked upon the *Slav Epic,* a historical fresco dedicated to the glory of his people.

The Slav postcards are a very different style than those of the French period. They are either panels from the *Slav Epic* or designs for fairs, spring celebrations, student festivals, or popular events. This was a patriotic period for Mucha. The only original postcard design in this group is *Emmahof Castle*. All others are taken from frescos or posters. §

Last sold for $13,500, April 1990

Rose Cecil O'Neill was born, June 25, 1874 in Wilkes Barre, Pennsylvania. Her father, William, wanted her to be an actress and taught her to recite Shakespeare. She absorbed the love of poetry from her father, who sold used books, especially poetry. Her mother, Alice, specialized in music and was a teacher. O'Neill learned to play piano pieces by Bach, Chopin and Schubert.

Never an exceptional financial provider, William O'Neill showered his family with the riches of culture. From Pennsylvania, her father moved the family to Nebraska where, at 14, O'Neill won a drawing competition sponsored by the *Omaha World Herald*. During the next two years, she did

illustrations and poems for the *Omaha World Herald* and the *Omaha Excelsior*.

By nineteen, she had written a novel. With this book and many drawings in her portfo-

lio, O'Neill traveled to New York. She stopped to see the World Columbian Exposition in Chicago where she saw, for the first time, the world of

modern painting and sculpture.

In New York, O'Neill attended the Convent of the Sisters of Saint Regis. She sold illustrations to *Truth*, *Collier's Weekly*, *Harper's Monthly*, and *Bazaar* to finance her education. While she was in New York, her father moved the family to the Ozark Mountains of Missouri.

When O'Neill returned home and saw Bonniebrook for the first time, her journey from the Springfield train station took two days by wagon. Today, the trip takes minutes.

Ruggles wrote in her book *One Rose*, "her heart became entangled with its charms, making her a willing slave to its allure for the rest of her life. It was her retreat when tired of

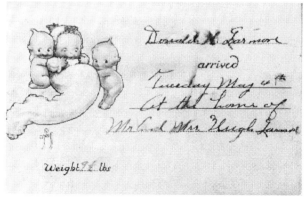

THE FIRST EDITION OF ALMOST

One Million

Klever Kards

HAS BEEN SOLD IN
LESS THAN TWO
MONTHS

ALMOST

Fifty Thousand Dollars

WORTH AT RETAIL

Some Business!!

Of Course You Are Selling Klever Kards

Catalog and sample for the asking

CAMPBELL ART CO., Elizabeth, N. J.

Wholesaler's Advertising

Harry Leon Wilson, and her personal collection.

O'Neill married Gray Latham in 1896. They lived in New York while she worked for *Puck*, signing her work O'Neill Latham and producing over 700 drawings. This marriage lasted five years. It is said the world knew of the impend-

the fast pace of city life, a haven of peace when her heart needed healing. She was a child of nature and everything about Bonniebrook enthralled her, feeding and making fruitful her imagination."

When she finally retired, Bonniebrook was the choice of all the places O'Neill had encountered. She brought pieces of her former homes with her, a fluted column from her home in New York, and a ten foot sculptured piece called, *The Embrace of the Tree,* which stood in the gardens of Carabas, O'Neill's home in Connecticut. The house was always overflowing with her father's books but she added her second husband's, noted playwright ing breakup before he did. When examining her work in *Puck*, we see the strong O'Neill-Latham signature turn into O'Neill with a "lazy L." She was phasing Mr. Latham out of her life and work.

O'Neill returned to Bonniebrook, where she received daily unsigned letters of affection from *Puck's* literary editor, Harry Leon Wilson. She had never formally met Wilson, but he had always admired her. When he heard of the divorce, he dreamed, what he thought was, the impossible dream. In 1902, Wilson left *Puck* and went to Bonniebrook to marry O'Neill. This marriage lasted six years, but she called him, even late in life, "The Beloved."

Again O'Neill returned to Bonniebrook to gain strength and hope for the future. This time she created the Kewpies. They first appeared in *Ladies' Home Journal,* in December of 1909. From this beginning, Kewpies appeared for nearly twenty five years in such publications as *Ladies' Home Journal*, *Woman's Home Companion*, *Good Housekeeping*, and *Delineator*. The first dolls were manufactured in Germany under the supervision of O'Neill and her sister, Callista. Because Rose was a smart business person, her Kewpie li-

censing for products produced over a million dollars. She also knew how to spend money. She expanded Bonniebrook to 8,000 square feet with modern conveniences like plumbing and electricity. Both of which were nearly unheard of in the Ozarks.

From 1912 to 1914, O'Neill stayed in Europe. With the war coming, she and Callista moved to Washington Square in New York City. They took two adjoining apartments and entertained friends, nonstop, for years. The song, *Rose of Washington Square* was written about Rose O'Neill.

In April of 1921, O'Neill had an exhibit of her *Sweet Monster* drawings at the Galerie Devambez in Paris. This exhibit gained her a position as an associate of the Societe des Beaux Arts. From France, O'Neill went to Spain, Italy and back to England. While in Italy she purchased the villa of Charles Coleman, with the understanding he was to stay as long as he lived. When Coleman died, he willed the contents to

O'Neill, which included many important works of art.

In 1925, O'Neill returned to New York and exhibited her *Sweet Monsters* in the Wildenstein galleries. From New York, the sisters went to Carabas Castle, near Westport, Connecticut. She had purchased this mansion in 1922. O'Neill had a huge steam boiler cast for this residence in the shape of a Kewpie.

At Carabas she created Scootles who first appeared in *The Ladies' Home Journal* in April, 1925. Scootles, like the Kewpies before her, was made into a doll after her print success. The soft Kuddle Kewpies were created at Carabas.

In 1936, O'Neill retired to Bonniebrook. She remarked, "I love this spot better than any place on earth." Here she wrote her autobiography, did illustration work and lectured on her life. In 1940, O'Neill created the Ho-Ho, a little laughing Buddha. She finished her memoirs, but died April 6, 1944 before they could be published.

O'Neill is buried in the family cemetery at Bonniebrook with her mother, brothers and sister. In 1947, Bonniebrook burned to the ground. Through the efforts of Kewpie collectors, the Bonniebrook Historical Society has rebuilt the house with exacting detail.

The Edward Gross Company published the first O'Neill Kewpie postcards. The cards, numbered 100-105 (shown in order) are scarce. The cards were flat printed in flesh tones on a gray-green background with cream borders.

Five of the six cards represent characters used in the first stories by O'Neill. *Kewpie Gardener* was added to this set. It was introduced in the *Ladies' Home Journal* by the September 1910 issue.

O'Neill did most of her postcards for Gibson Art Co. and Campbell Art Co. The Campbell Art Klever Kards are more desirable than the Gibsons. Raphael Tuck reproduced the Black non-Kewpie images she did for *Puck* magazine. These cards are scarce. The baby birth announcement and the ice cream advertising cards are rare. §

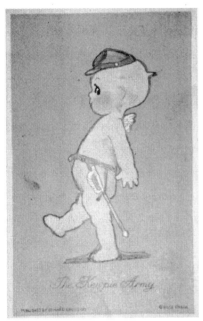

The Kewpie Army

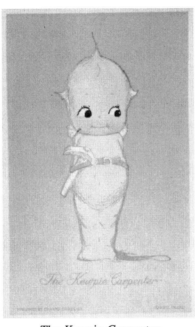

The Kewpie Carpenter

This Kewpie wears Overshoes

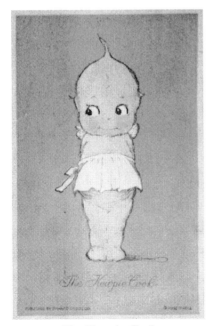

The Kewpie Cook

This Kewpie's careful of his Voice

The Kewpie Gardener

The Encyclopedia of Antique Postcards

OPPER

Frederick Burr Opper was born in Madison, Ohio, in 1857. He left school at the age of fourteen, which was not uncommon for that era, and went to work for the *Madison Gazette* newspaper.

He did free-lance cartoons for *Scribner's*, *The Century Magazine*, and *St. Nicholas*. Opper moved to New York when he was 19, taking a position with the magazine *Wild*

Just Been to the Races.

Oats, but continued free-lance cartoon work for *Puck* and *Harper's Bazaar*.

When Colonel Frank Leslie started his new magazine,

Leslie's, in 1877, he hired Opper as a news reporter, cartoonist and illustrator. After three years with *Leslie's* magazine, Opper went to work as the lead cartoonist for *Puck* magazine.

William Randolph Hearst hired Opper, at the age of 42, to do weekly cartoons for Hearst's *American Humorists*, a section of the New York *Journal*. The dean emeritus of the American comic strip, Opper never produced daily comic strip work. During the first 15 years of the new century, he produced three full page and several half page Sunday episodes each week. The syndicated system of Hearst Publishing carried the work of Opper in newspapers throughout the world.

Opper's talents extended beyond cartoons with book illustrations for *Samantha At Saratoga*, *Bailed Hay*, *Our Antediluvian Ancestors*, *The Folks In Funnyville*, and *Up to Date Conundrums*.

His best remembered and loved character, Happy Hooligan, made its first appearance on March 26, 1900. He was a round faced

I merely wish to remark

Valentine Greetings

tramp, who immediately captured the hearts of the public. This character was followed by equally successful *Alphonse and Gaston* and *Maud the Mule*.

In 1932, Opper retired because of failing eyesight. He

WE'RE BEATING ALL RECORDS

Just a Few Words.

died on August 28, 1937 in his home in New Rochelle, NY. §

I am happy to say

The most sought after DuPont advertising cards are the series of 13 championship hunting dogs. Edmond H. Osthaus, Toledo, did the postcards and the original paintings of the National Field Trial winners from 1896 to 1910. He was born 1858, died 1928.

The advertising message is very simple, "Shoot DuPont Powders." Copyrighted June 1916, the set was available from the Advertising Division of DuPont and Company, Wilmington, Delaware, for ten cents (U.S.) or fifteen cents (Canadian) postpaid. A cover card was included in the set which listed all thirteen titles.

The DuPont Powder Wild Game series is more common, yet desirable. The twelve cards in this set consist of: *Blue Wing Teal*, *Pair of Mallards*, *Canada Goose*, *Prairie Chicken*, *Can-* *vass Backs*, *Quail*, *Gray Squirrel*, *Ruffed Grouse*, *Jack Rabbit*, *Wild Turkey*, *Jack Snipe* and *Woodcock*. §

Edm. H. Osthaus

Count Gladstone IV - 1896

Tony's Gale - 1898

Joe Cumming - 1899

Lady's Count Gladstone - 1900

Sioux - 1901, 1902

Geneva - 1903

Mohawk II - 1904

Allambagh - 1905

Pioneer - 1906

Prince Whitestone - 1907

Count Whitestone II - 1908

Manitoba Rap - 1909

Monora 1910

The Encyclopedia of Antique Postcards

Buster Brown, with his two friends,
This jolly old saint assails.
Old "Santa Claus", we know you well,
You come from BLOOMINGDALES.
3rd to Lexington Aves. 59th to 60th Sts.

While Buster Brown is at the grip,
He lets no good occasion slip,
To give advice that never fails
"All cars transfer to BLOOMINGDALES."
3rd to Lexington Aves. 59th to 60th Sts.

When Buster Brown met Daisy Lee
Twas where we sell "ze lingerie"
A place where dainty bargains are
At BLOOMINGDALES, take any car.
3rd to Lexington Aves. 59th to 60th Sts.

Richard Felton Outcault was born on January 14, 1863 in Lancaster, Ohio. He studied art at McMicken University in Cincinnati. On Christmas Day, 1890, he married Mary Jane Martin and moved to Long Island, New York.

He came from a wealthy family and was a free-lance cartoonist for *Life*, *Judge*, *Truth* and the New York *World*. For the *World*, Outcault created the first page of cartoons to be printed in color. The series, *Hogan's Alley*, featured a small bald child in a yellow night-shirt, the Yellow Kid. Outcault never gave the child that name. The public and Hearst did, when he hired Outcault away from the *World*.

The combination of Hearst's sensationalist journalism and the flashy *Yellow Kid* series, led to the term Yellow Journalism. Outcault hated the squabbling the comic page caused between the two papers. He dropped the *Yellow Kid* and created for the *Herald, Poor Li'l Mose*. This black child, featured in caricature, didn't carry the interest of the *Yellow Kid* and Outcault replaced him with *Buster Brown* in 1902. The models for Buster Brown and Mary Jane were his two children.

Buster Brown's balance between hell raising and propriety didn't offend Outcault's social circle. He was a healthy boy dressed in a way parents found attractive, and copied for their children's clothing.

Outcault wisely controlled the rights to his characters and by 1905 was earning more by producing clothing and artifacts than from the comic strip.

A wealthy man by 1910, Outcault treated *Buster* as a hobby, which he finally gave up in 1920, though the reprints continued until 1926. He gave the Outcault Advertising Company of Chicago to his son when he retired. He died on September 25, 1928, at the age of 65. Outcault was hailed as the "father of the modern newspaper supplement."

Buster Brown and Tige appeared in newspapers, books, advertising premiums and on postcards. Hearst's Sunday newspapers issued sheets of postcards that the readers cut apart. McIntosh published a ten card set, titled *Buster Brown and his Bubble*. Tuck, Tammen and Ullman published many Outcault postcards.

The rarest postcard sets of Outcault's work feature the Yellow Kid character. These elusive cards usually are from the calendar series and no complete set featuring the Yellow Kid has been found.

The rarest Buster Brown postcards by Outcault are the six card set issued by Bloomingdale's department store of New York as advertising premiums. (See Yellow Kid for more Outcault.) §

R. F. Outcault

Milton Dressing Figure Series 602 Woolstone Brothers of London

To be considered a paper doll, the figure must have a change of outfit. This lucky fellow has six outfits, for roles as hunter, jockey, sailor, police officer, fire fighter and life boat rescuer.

This postcard set, after escaping the clutches of a child with scissors, has remained unused and mint for over 50 years.

This type of postcard was generally produced just before and during the 1920s. Postcard collecting, as a fad, was disappearing. Louis Wain designed the most expensive paper toy postcards of this type (see Wain).

PAPER TOYS

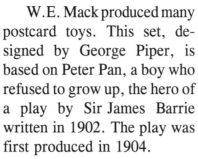

W.E. Mack produced many postcard toys. This set, designed by George Piper, is based on Peter Pan, a boy who refused to grow up, the hero of a play by Sir James Barrie written in 1902. The play was first produced in 1904.

The lead characters: Peter, Hook, the Indian, Wendy, Nana, and the Crocodile are subjects of this *Toy Town* series, No. 094. The individual cards are numbered 094-099. As the envelope indicates, the series number of the first card denotes the packet number. The cards are mechanical toys that assemble with paper fasteners or string (results, right).

Designed by George Piper

Toy Town Series 094-099 by W. E. Mack London

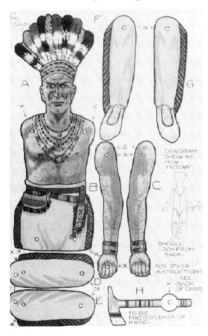

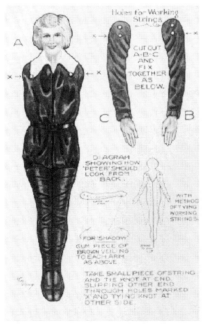

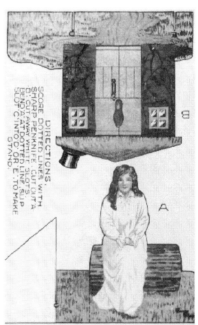

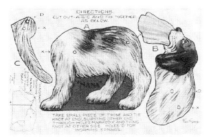

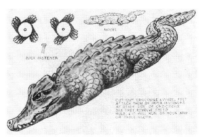

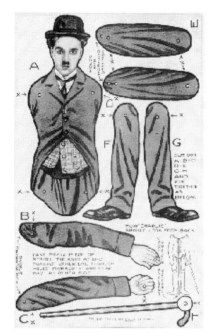

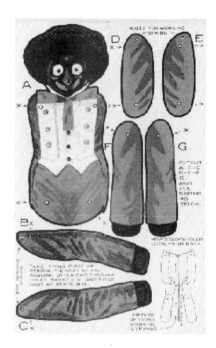

W. E. Mack
Series
052

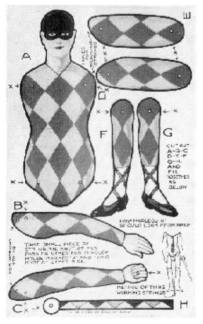

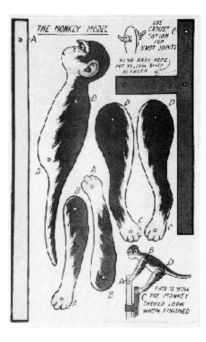

*Brothers and Sisters, 6 Dolls
for painting, cutting & dressing*

*Interior of Box at left
paints, paper dolls & postcards*

S & Company
Series
351

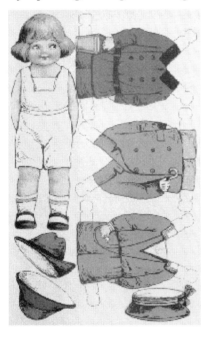

PAPER TOYS

George Borgfeldt and Co. was the sole agent for the Fletcher paper toys of New York. J. Alan Fletcher's signature was the trademark.

The three books illustrated were copyrighted 1915, but individual cards within the book are copyrighted both 1914 and 1915. Each of the eight cards is oversized, approximately four inches by six inches. Not all Fletchers are oversized.

Each individual card is numbered. The Mother Goose Rhymes is numbered: 19-24, 37, 38. The Housekeeping and Dolls series is numbered: 25-27, 35, 36, 39, 41, 43. The Alice Around the World series is numbered: 31-34, 40, 42, 44, 45.

There were six books of this type, according to the back cover: 1) *Alice Around the World*, 2) *Housekeeping and Dolls*, 3) *Mother Goose Rhymes*, 4) *Fire Engines and Trains*, 5) *Bronchos and Aeroplanes*, 6) *U.S. and European Soldiers*.

These six books contained the oversized versions of 48 postcards. The cards were also produced in standard size; while neither size is common, the

176

PAPER TOYS

21. This Little Pig
22. Humpty Dumpty, All the Kings Horses
23. The Old Woman Who Lived in the Shoe
24. Simple Simon Met a Pie Man
25. Mabel Cooking, Toy Kitchen
26. Mabel at Dinner
27. Mabel at Toy Piano
28. Circus Horse, Two Soldiers and an Indian
29 Automobile and Driver
30. Elephant and Three Riders
31. Romola, Italian
32. Alice, American
33. San Toy, Chinese
34. Butterfly, Japanese
35. Maria, Hungarian
36. Katrina, Dutch

Numbers 37-48 copyrighted 1915
37. Peter Pan Pumpkin Eater
38. Three Wise Men of Gotham
39. Put Dolly & Teddy to Bed
40. Alice Travelling
41. Alice at Dressing Table
42. Alice at the Seashore
43. Alice at the Hat Store
44. Alice with Camel and Trainer
45. Alice in the Gondola
46. Broncho Wildfire
47. Hook and Ladder
48. Fire Engine §

standard cards have survived most often.

The following checklist is for the Fletchers by number, not by book series:

Numbers 1-36 copyrighted 1914
1. Austrian Soldiers
2. Seaplane with four pilots: German, French, Russian and English.
3. Unknown (probably book 6)
4. Unknown (probably book 6)
5. English Mounted Infantry
6. Paper Soldiers, The German Guards
7. Russians in Action
8. United States Regulars
9. French on the Firing Line (with bike)
10. Mexican
11. Scotch Highlanders
12. Unknown (probably book 6)
13. Ship
14. Build the Steamship, Aquitania
15-17 Unknown (probably book 4)
18. Ridgewood Railroad Depot, water tank, Signal Tower, Hand car.
19. Hey! Diddle Diddle
20. King Have a Heart

Studio Portrait

Horse Drawn Merchant Wagon

George Eastman, in 1888, produced a simple box camera with 100 exposures of film preloaded. When exposed, it was returned to the factory complete for developing. By 1902, Kodak sold photographic paper with preprinted postcard backs, allowing cards to be made directly from negatives. Between 1906 and 1910, Kodak printed postcards for amateurs.

This type of card, because of its limited supply, is the nearest thing to one of a kind postcards. This uniqueness, combined with its historic significance, is why real photographic cards are so highly collected. These postcards often shed more light on the social and political development of the past than any other source. The photo postcards are actual glimpses out of time.

Postcards record the growth of a town, the birth of its citizenry and even their deaths. When the train went off the bridge, the fierce winter storm dumped two feet of snow, the streets flooded, the barn burned, or the building collapsed, it was photographed and made into a postcard.

Through postcards, a raging blizzard, that started in the West and traveled to the East coast, can be documented. Postmarked cards from the cities in the storm's path tell the speed, the messages the amount of snowfall, and the photographs of how each town looked after the storm. §

Amateur Photo Postcard

Interior of Meat Market

PIGS

This delightful set tells the story of a pig family going to market to fetch fresh produce and eggs. Like any family starting on a great adventure, everyone is in good spirits. The wagon is loaded with empty baskets and piglets. At the market, mother selects a variety of healthy goods, including eggs, which she decides to hand carry, to no avail. When the donkey stumbles throwing produce and baby pigs in all directions, the eggs join the losses.

This is an example of a set telling a story. Often these were sent one each day. While each card may have visual appeal, it is not until the set is complete that the whole story is known.

Pigs have been a symbol of good luck for centuries. They are featured on many New Year's Day cards with four-leaf clovers and horseshoes.

The best pig postcards are chromo lithographed on high quality paper stock with an outstanding design. The most sought after images show dressed pigs doing human activities. The hold to light pig cards, the installment pig cards, and the pigs of Arthur Thiele are the most desirable. §

POLITICAL

Major Candidates
1900 McKinley vs. Bryan
1904 Roosevelt vs. Parker
1908 Taft vs. Bryan
1912 Wilson vs. Taft
1916 Wilson vs. Hughes
1920 Harding vs. Cox
1924 Coolidge vs. Davis
1928 Hoover vs. Smith
1932 Roosevelt vs. Hoover
1936 Roosevelt vs. Landon
1940 Roosevelt vs. Willkie
1944 Roosevelt vs. Dewey
1948 Truman vs. Dewey

Gone is the idea of being picked to be President. The original idea was for electors, chosen by individual state legislatures, to meet and cast their vote for President; the runner up was made Vice President.

That process lasted until 1800, when the idea of campaigning began, not by the candidate but by his friends. It was considered in very poor taste for the candidate to take part; while it was acceptable to serve when called upon.

This changed again with the campaign of 1896, when McKinley and Bryan took their positions directly to the people. Bryan made railroad tours from Nebraska to the East Coast delivering over 600 speeches. McKinley stayed in Canton, Ohio, receiving thousands of travelers, while sitting on his front porch.

180

POLITICAL

The significant change, in terms of collecting, was that for the first time, there was a paper trail. Each candidate produced posters and editorial pamphlets aimed at "getting the vote." In the age of no telephones, radio, television and few daily newspapers, the mail became a super medium. By the election of 1900, the postcard was seen as a tool "to get the message out." Today, the campaign cards, before 1908, are scarce.

In 1908, postcard collecting was all the craze and the campaign cards from this era are abundant. Political campaign cards fall into two groups, those produced by party organizations to promote their candidate and those produced by postcard publishers to sell postcards. The most commonly found postcards are from this last group.

A set might consist of six cards for a candidate and six cards against the same candidate. Bigger publishers had the means to produce thousands of humorous cards, while smaller companies were more conservative. The more produced; the more likely they survived.

The political parties produced the most sought after cards. These include either jugate cards that show the running pair, President and Vice President, or real photo cards with the candidate on the campaign trail. The rarest in this group are the cards of "off beat" candidates, like those of Eugene Debs running on the Socialist Party ticket.

As a rule of thumb, postcards of Democratic candidates are harder to find than those of Republican candidates, with off beat parties harder yet. Some candidates to watch for are Eugene Debs, Socialist Party; Eugene Chafin, Prohibition Party; and the jugate cards of Roosevelt and Johnson running on the Progressive Party ticket in 1912.

Periolat copyrighted this set of postcards in 1910. Designed and signed by the artist, Seed, they depict Roosevelt's return from Africa. Disgusted with Taft's performance, he threw his hat into the 1912 political ring only to be rejected by his party. He ran that year on a Progressive party ticket, but the split vote threw the election to Wilson. §

Julia Wades in the Water

Wades in the Water

Winold Reiss, born in 1888, came to America to paint Indians, leaving Germany in 1913. He expected to be greeted by Indians on the docks of New York. It would be six years before his dream of painting Indians would be fulfilled.

While in New York City, he devoted his time to commercial art. He designed the interior of the *Busy Lady Bakery*, and the first American art deco restaurant, *The Crillon.*

His first Indian painting was of a Blackfoot he found in New York. For props, Reiss borrowed a war bonnet and beaded shirt from the American Museum of National History. In 1919, Reiss and one of his students rode the Great Northern Railway to the Blackfoot Nation in Montana.

The Indians were not allowed to leave the reservation, but he arrived in time to capture the identity of the Blackfeet before their symbols and traditions were lost. The first Indian he met was *Angry Bull*. They became lifelong friends.

Reiss shared a local Montana hotel room with a cowboy who used the bed during the day, while Reiss trudged to the reservation to paint his Indians. The Blackfeet initiated him into the tribe, naming him *Beaver Child*, because of his hard work. In 30 days, Reiss created 35 portraits. The Indians recognized that he "wanted to record their greatness, not just for himself but for THEM." They trusted Reiss and willingly revealed their coveted lives, dressing in their war paint and finery.

In 1920, he exhibited at the Hanfstaengl Gallery, in New York. Dr. Phillip Cole purchased all the paintings, now in the Bradford Brinton Museum in Big Horn, Montana.

It would be eight years before Reiss would return to Montana. During this time, he created portraits of the Afro-Americans of Harlem. He wanted to record Harlem's history, featuring Black lawyers, college students, singers, and teachers. When he finished this endeavor in 1925, no gallery in New York would exhibit his work. The Harlem Branch Library mounted the show.

Alain Locke, a Black essayist, wrote of the show, "Winold Reiss has achieved what amounts to a revealing discovery of the significance, human and artistic, of one of the great dialects of human physiognomy." Today, 12 of these paintings are in the collection of the Smithsonian's National Portrait Gallery.

By mid-1920 Hans Reiss, Winold's brother and a sculptor, arrived in New York, but the summer heat forced Hans to Glacier National Park, where he became a mountain guide. Hans met Louis Hill, president of the Great Northern Railway. This meeting landed a commission for Winold to paint the Blackfoot Indians in Montana and Alberta. Starting in the summer of 1927, he painted the Indians every summer until the beginning of World War II.

The Great Northern Railway paid for Reiss' trips to the West. Hill purchased 80 of Reiss' paintings, and others were reproduced on calendars,

REISS

menus and postcards. Today, the Burlington Northern Railway and Hill's heirs still own most of these paintings.

Reiss never romanticized the Indian. He simply and clearly recorded the character of the individuals. It is remarkable that Reiss recorded almost all the people of one tribe.

During the winters, Reiss did commercial work consisting of postcards of restaurants. Reiss designed the interior of the chain called *Longchams*. Reiss designed early 30 hotels, theaters, taverns, offices and cafes, in New York, Chicago and Boston. He designed matchbox covers, menus, and logos for restaurant trucks. His largest commission was the Cincinnati, Ohio, Union Terminal that opened in 1933.

Trained in Munich, Germany, by Julius Diez and Franz von Stuck, the famed teachers of Paul Klee and Wassily Kandinsky, Reiss fell from favor during the 1940s because of growing anti-German sentiment among many important clients. On August 29, 1953, Reiss died of a stroke. His son, Tjark Reiss, sent his father's ashes to a Blackfoot Indian named Bull Child. Tjark learned later, Bull Child collected all who remembered the artist "on a day when the winds played tricks, they gathered on Red Blanket Hill, at whose feet the cottonwoods were shedding. Here, at last, with the old Blackfeet Nation in attendance, the ashes were scattered. The high winds took them far." §

WINOLD REISS

Angry Bull

Mountain Flower

Middle Rider

Lazy Boy

Sundance

Clears Up

The Sign Talkers

Tom Dawson

The Encyclopedia of Antique Postcards

Norman Rockwell's first cover for *Saturday Evening Post* was May 20, 1916. Because the magazine was so popular, many feel he did all the covers, but he did only 323 of the nearly 4,000 covers.

His work spans many magazine covers, advertisers, calendars, portraits, and a mural for the Nassau Tavern of Princeton, New Jersey, which is illustrated on a two panel postcard.

The architect of that Princeton building, Tom Stapleton, ask Rockwell to do the mural. The painting took nine months in his studio. The original was thirteen feet long. Rockwell researched the costumes and made them for his models to wear.

It was not easy to scale up his work from magazine format to a wall size canvas. Rockwell's paintings were full of action, avoided by most mural artists. Rockwell, managed to stop the racing eye of the viewer by putting the hitching post and decorative ribbon across the feet of the boy, dog, goose and pony. Another brake to the rapid movement was the clever device of the boy pulling on the horse's tail.

Norman Rockwell

The other Rockwell postcards are for Sanford's Ink and the Upjohn Company of Kalamazoo, Michigan. The boy with his dog was a sales representatives card mailed in 1941.

The Upjohn Company started in 1936 to become a patron of the arts, purchasing original art from American painters. These paintings by Simkhovitch, Pierce, Davis, Conrow, Koch, Clemens, Anderson and Binford dramatized important health issues in Upjohn ads. The copy was written to fit the picture instead of hiring an illustrator to match the words. In 1946, the paintings made a cross country tour of museums. They were then placed on public exhibition as a permanent collection of contemporary American art. §

SCHMUCKER

This National Art Company series by Samuel Schmucker depicts a soldier's enthusiasm for letters from home. These postcards were some of Schmucker's last work before his death in 1921.

THREE CHEERS AND HIP HIP HOORAY A LETTER CAME FROM YOU TODAY!

Letters from Home

A LETTER A DAY KEEPS THE BLUES AWAY

WHEN TIME HANGS HEAVY ON MY HANDS AND EVERYTHING SEEMS BLUE THERES NOTHING QUITE AS WELCOME AS A NICE LONG LETTER FROM YOU

OH! LET THIS DREAM COME TRUE

I WASNT SO HAPPY LAST NIGHT BUT TODAY ...

WHEN OF ME YOU SOMETIMES THINK GO RIGHT FOR THE PEN AND INK THERE IS NOTHING SUITS US BETTER THAN TO GET A NEWSY LETTER.

YOUR LETTER TODAY WAS A TREAT THAT I HOPE YOU WILL OFTEN REPEAT IT MAKES ME FEEL FINE WHEN YOU DROP ME A LINE FOR THE LETTERS YOU WRITE CANT BE BEAT

A LETTER FROM YOU LOOKS BIG AS THIS TO ME

YOU SEND ME ONE WITH A SMILE IF ... LETTERS YOULL WRITE ME A PILE IT GIVES ME THE BLUES NOT TO GET ANY NEWS SO PLEASE WRITE ME ONCE IN A WHILE

Mottoes
Gather Ye Rose-buds as Ye May,
Old Time is Still a Flying.
Detroit Publishing Company
Numbers 14659-14664

Any information that collectors have about Samuel L. Schmucker, is due to the relentless research of Dottie Ryan and George Miller for their book, *Picture Postcards in the United States*. While in Washington, D.C., Miller discovered the designs of Schmucker, as he searched the files of the Winsch copyrights.

Baby Days - I

The Runaway - II

Playtime - III

Schmucker was a resident of Wilmington, Deleware, and a student of the Pennsylvania Academy of the Fine Arts from 1896-1899. He was born February 20, 1879 and died September 4, 1921. He signed some of his postcard work with the monogram SLS. §

Childhood Days
Ah! what would the world be to us
If the children were no more?
Detroit Publishing Company

Among the Flowers - IV

Fairy Tales - V

Off to School - VI

Creating thousands of drawings and hundreds of oil paintings, Jessie Wilcox Smith captured the tender moments of a mother's touch, the texture of a flower between tiny fingers and the unending curiosity of a child.

Smith's first published illustration was a simple line drawing for *Saint Nicholas* magazine in 1888. Her first illustration, using the style that was to become distinctly hers, was published in 1901.

The transformation in styles took place after her studies with Howard Pyle, the Dean of American illustration, at the Drexel Institute of Art and Science. Pyle may have sparked the creativity of Smith, but more importantly, he supplied her with many contacts needed to succeed in the publishing field.

In 1901, Smith and Elizabeth Shippen Green produced a self-invested calendar, featuring the most beautiful work either artist had ever created. They immortalized small children at play. This became the turning point in Smith's career. Stokes, a New York publishing house, asked permission to reprint the calendar with poems in book form. It was titled, *The Book of the Child*.

In 1902, Smith gained national attention, when she was awarded the bronze medal for painting from the International Charleston, South Carolina, Exposition. Additional formal recognition came in 1903, when Smith received the Mary Smith Award from the Academy. Smith continued to enter her work in competitions. In 1915, she won the watercolor medal at the Panama Pacific International Exposition in San Francisco. That year, she completed one of her most important series of illustrations for a book written by Charles Kingley, titled *Water Babies*.

After the book, other offers of work deluged Smith. She signed a contract with *Good Housekeeping* magazine that lasted for fifteen years. She designed every cover for *Good Housekeeping* from December 1917 through March 1933. Besides *Good Housekeeping*, she illustrated covers for *Collier's Weekly*, *Harper's Young People*,

Delineator, *McClure's Magazine*, *Woman's Home Companion*, and *Scribner's*. Her great success was based on the fact, it was a rare mother who could not identify with Smith's drawings.

During the 1920s, she devoted much of her time to portrait work. Smith could produce nearly one dozen portraits each year, besides her illustration assignments. Her portrait fees were high at $500 to $1,000 each.

Smith illustrated more than forty books, hundreds of magazine covers, articles and advertisements. Her advertising illustrations included work for Ivory Soap, Cuticura Soap, Kodak camera, American Radiator and Campbell's Soup.

Smith was born on September 3, 1863 in Philadelphia, Pennsylvania, the youngest of four children. She studied to be a kindergarten teacher, one of few professions open to women, and taught briefly.

When she died, in 1936, the *New York Times* wrote, "The children that Miss Smith painted were reflective and a little sedate and in her art the maternal note predominated. She seemed haunted by the vision of two

POST CARDS.

JESSIE WILLCOX SMITH SERIE
(Child in Garden).

SET OF SIX CARDS.

REINTHAL & NEWMAN,   CHARLES HAUFF,
NEW YORK.   LONDON.

SMITH

faces, and the face of one was the face of a mother." Smith remained unmarried her entire life.

In 1903, Smith illustrated the December issue of *Scribner's* magazine. The series, *The Child in a Garden*, was later used for post card

series number 100, published by Reinthal and Newman. This six card set has full signatures.

JESSIE WILLCOX SMITH

Another postcard of Smith's features a child pulling petals from a daisy, *She Lufs Me -- She Lufs Me Not*. This illustration

was taken from the June 29, 1907 *Collier's* magazine cover. In 1911, the same illustration was published in *The Now-a-Days Fairy Book*. This postcard was cropped, resulting in a partial signature of MITH. Smith never created any work just for postcards. §

The Garden Wall

In the Garden

The Green Door

The Lily Pool

Among the Poppies

Five O'clock Tea

The Encyclopedia of Antique Postcards

189

STATE GIRLS

There were many sets issued relating to states, such as state capitols, state belles, state flowers and state girls. They were published by Langsdorf, National Art Company, Raphael Tuck, and Platinachrome. Some are artist signed, like the National Art set by St. John.

Generally, these sets contained 45 postcards, one for each state in the Union during the Golden Age. The most desirable set is the one published by the firm Samuel Langsdorf located in New York. They issued thirty cards featuring beautiful women for AR, CA, CO, CT, FL, GA, IL, IN, IA, KS, KY, LA, MD, ME, MA, MI, MS, MO, NE, NJ, NY, OH, OR, PA, TX, VT, VA, WA, WV, and WI. Each card was designed in the United States and sent to Germany for printing. This resulted in exceptional color quality.

The postcards were published both flat and embossed; with and without state names; applied silk on the costumes; or scored to create puzzles.

The puzzle cards were issued with envelopes, but have postcard backs. The sender was to write a message on the card, tear it apart and mail it. The receiver had to solve the puzzle to read the message. They were very clever, but very few of these cards survived as a result.

Each Langsdorf state girl postcard has, as the background, the shield and coat of arms of her corresponding state. The costumes of the women are symbolic of the individual states.

The puzzle postcards are the hardest to find, followed by the silks. The regular postcards are available, but certain states are hard to find. Those states that are hardest to find, are usually smaller in size or sparsely populated. Collectors often mix sets. §

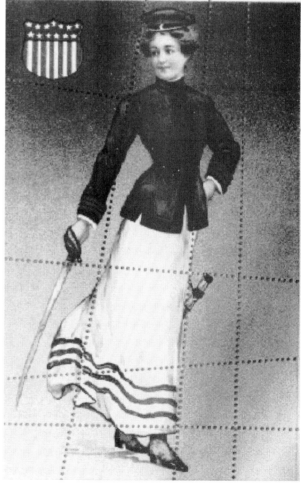

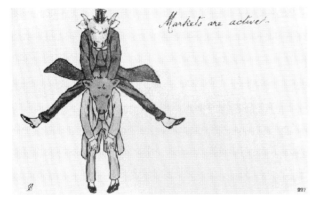

Stock Market history begins in Antwerp, Belgium, in 1531. It wasn't until 1773, that London formed its stock exchange. In New York City, brokers were meeting under an old buttonwood tree on Wall Street. It was these street entrepreneurs who, in 1792, formed the New York Stock Exchange. The American Stock Exchange was formed in 1849.

The stock exchanges are marketplaces, where member-brokers buy and sell stocks and bonds for the public. These investments provided companies with a flood of new capital for business expansion.

Considering its two century history in England and America, one would think the stock market would have been a subject for many postcards. Yet, very little material exists. This English set has a divided back with a half penny stamp box and a series number 227.

The bull symbolizes an active market; the bear indicates a slow market. The bull leaps over the bear with a caption, *Markets are Active*. The bull and bear battle on *Pay Day*. When the market slows, the bull shows his empty pockets and comments, *A Slump, we've got no work to do-oo-oo*. Market dealings with China and a 20 percent dividend being fired upon England by Uncle Sam, reflected the times. §

STUDDY

The artist, George Studdy was born on June 23, 1878. He attended evening classes at Heatherley's and one term at Calderon's Animal School, where he learned anatomy. Bonzo is not any particular dog, but a combination of various traits of several breeds.

Friday nights, the London Sketch Club held drawing classes with critiques. Studdy belonged to many of these artist clubs, where he learned and grew in his craft.

The sale of his first drawings was a great delight. At 15 cents each, it meant he could maintain a modest life style.

By 1912, Studdy had a formidable reputation as an illustrator and cartoonist. His work appeared in, *The Tatler*, *The Bystander*, *The Graphic*, *The Sketch* and the *Illustrated London News*. He married Blanche Landrin and settled in London.

A dog appeared in his work over the years, but the first dog, that had any of the Bonzo personality, he drew for *Pearson's Magazine*. The drawing depicted a hound running with a wasp sitting on its tail.

During World War I, Studdy developed his character, Bonzo. After the war,

Sketch gave him a six month trial of *The Studdy Dog*. It was a great success and the series continued for many years.

On November 8th, 1922, *Sketch* editor, Bruce Ingram named the dog Bonzo. Studdy didn't like it. He lacked the desire to name a dog Bonzo, but he did have several cocker spaniels, all named Ben. His wife had many Pekinese, all named Chee Kee. This dog became Bonzo's girlfriend.

Studdy continued to have great success with his work, appearing on the London art gallery circuit, and in 1923 exhibited work at the Walker

JUST TO AMUSE YOU

WHAT ABOUT A BEER AT THE POLE DUCKY?

Gallery. The fame of Bonzo made the Studdy family financially secure.

Bonzo was featured among the first neon signs in Piccadilly Circus, London's answer to Time Square. The memorabilia, created and sold to the public beyond the published page, started in the early 1920s. *The Sketch* issued a series of six portfolios of Bonzo cartoons. The first appeared in 1922. They were issued until 1925; when the last one, *Bonzo's Star Turns*, completed the set.

There were perfume bottles, ink wells, egg cups, jugs, pots, ashtrays and condiment sets. Both Royal Doulton and Royal Worcester produced the best pieces in porcelain. Spears of Enfield produced several Bonzo based games. Both Deans Rag Book Company and Chad Valley made stuffed toys of Bonzo.

Bonzo made his stage debut in Jack Buchanan's pro-

duction of *Battling Butler* in 1923. Then, Bonzo moved to the movie screen with a series of 26 cartoons. Studdy, with ten other artists, worked day and night to create thousands of drawings. The first film was shown on October 14, 1924, attended by King George V and Queen Mary; the first time a reigning monarch had watched a film in a public theater.

Bonzo went international, when he was syndicated in

NOT HAVING TOO BAD A TIME!

"JUST 'COS I HAVEN'T HEARD FROM YOU."

Wildt and Kray, and several other publishers.

Deans published Bonzo Annuals, which first appeared in 1935. Though Studdy died on July 25th, 1948, the annuals continued until 1952. §

several newspapers in the United States, India, South Africa and South America. In Europe, his books, advertisements and postcards were translated to many languages.

His main postcard publisher, Valentine of Dundee, kept him busy creating well over 500 different designs. He worked for Gale and Polden, James Henderson, Inter-Art, J. Salmon, Milton, W.E. Mack,

YOU ARE MY ONE AND ONLY LITTLE CAVEMAN!

I QUEEN DREAM OF YOU.

SUFFRAGE

ELECTION—DAY

I DON'T CARE

I LOVE MY HUSBAND BUT—
OH YOU VOTE

·SUFFRAGETTE MADONNA·

QUEEN OF THE POLL

WHERE, OH WHERE IS MY
WANDERING WIFE TONIGHT?

It wasn't until 1920 that the 19th Amendment granting women the voting franchise became law in the United States. It was 80 years after an effort to seat women delegates from the United States at a World Antislavery Convention in London and 72 years after the first woman suffrage convention in Seneca Falls, New York.

Elizabeth Cady Stanton and Lucretia Mott led the first convention and, shortly after that, Lucy Stone in 1850 called a women's rights convention at Worcester, Massachusetts. These meetings excited much public discussion and during the next ten years other women joined the crusade.

Susan B. Anthony, with

Elizabeth Stanton, founded the National Woman Suffrage Association in 1869 to oppose the 15th Amendment, which granted the right to vote to Black men, but not women. During the same period, the American Woman Suffrage Association tried to persuade the states, rather than the federal government, to grant the

194

franchise to women. The two organizations joined forces in 1890, as the National American Woman Suffrage Association. Four states granted state suffrage to women during that decade, Wyoming (1890), Colorado (1893), Utah (1896) and Idaho (1896).

The postcard artists of the period often designed both pro-suffrage and anti-suffrage cards for the publishers. Sometimes identical motifs were published with different messages, one pro and one con.

In 1909, the Dunston-Weiler Lithograph Company of New York produced this set of 12 comic cards dealing with Woman Suffrage. The set was produced with both gold and white backgrounds, so the collector must watch carefully to obtain one set or the other. Mixed cards are illustrated here to show the difference, but the images are identical.

The strongest image of the series is number 6, *Uncle Sam, Suffragee*. These cards are visually interesting, with vivid coloring and active designs.

UNCLE SAM. SUFFRAGEE.

·SUFFRAGETTE· COPPETTE·
BEWARE OF THE DOG

I WANT TO VOTE. BUT
MY·WIFE·WONT·LET·ME

ELECTIONEERING

PANTALETTE SUFFRAGETTE
IN THE SWEET BYE AND BYE

SUFFRAGETTE VOTE-GETTING
THE EASIEST WAY.

Suffrage cards are always highly desirable. During the Golden Age of postcards (1893-1918), many important political and social issues were depicted photographically and by satirical drawings on cards. Postcard publishers took every opportunity to exploit the anti-suffrage side of the feminist movement and the *Votes for Women* campaign.

The comic postcards of this early time became the tool of the anti-suffrage campaign. These cards portrayed women as absent from the home, while parading for woman's rights. Fathers were shown in such unmanly chores as caring for the children, washing the clothes, scrubbing floors and missing their much deserved night out with the boys.

Though most cards were heavily anti-suffrage, some were pro-suffrage. When the pro-suffrage cards are found today, they usually have not been postally used. Perhaps the social climate was such that these cards were hand exchanged or merely kept by the purchaser.

Ellam designed this colorful six postcard English set, numbered 946, for Misch and Company. (See Ellam for more information.) §

SUNBONNETS

Ullman Manufacturing Company

Sunday	1860
Monday	1861
Tuesday	1862
Wednesday	1863
Thursday	1864
Friday	1865
Saturday	1866

Arthur Thiele is praised for his ability to instill human-like qualities into animals. The most common examples of his work feature cats and dogs portraying human events; typical, is an old fashioned classroom with misbehaving students.

His cats could sing, knit, go to church and skip rope. While his postcards of cats are the most appealing, he produced humorous postcard sets, featuring musicians and public beach scenes.

Not much is known about the artist, but Garnier and Lluch report in *Cartes postales d'illustrateurs* that he was born 1841, died in 1916 and was of German origin. Theo. Stroefer, of Nuremberg (TSN), published most of Thiele's work with numbers from 700 to 2500.

His early work features a single animal image; while his later work shows busy scenes of confusion with many animal images on a single card.

Thiele was a prolific artist, who worked until he was in his 70s. Many of his later sets were produced on a coarse,

cream colored paper stock, with poor printing quality.

Arthur Thiele's set, series number 995, published by T.S.N. features kittens playing Cupid. Each kitten has wings of either birds, moths, butterflies or dragonflies. The quivers holding their arrows are elaborately, trimmed in gold and held by ribbons.

Cats have been appealing subjects over the centuries. Many famous artists have sung about, written about and illustrated their antics. Postcard artists continued the tradition started by advertising trade card artists.

As if cats were not attractive enough, many artists went a step further and dressed them as people. Thiele captured the collector's heart with his set numbered 1424 published by Theo Stroefer of Nurenberg, Germany. It is one of few sets that Thiele created with oversized cat heads.

Thiele portrayed cats in the act of dastardly deeds, which bring a smile to your face when you look into those cat eyes. §

FIrth. Thiele

G. A. Novelty
Art Series
TSN 789

THIELE

ARTH.THIELE

TSN
871

The Encyclopedia of Antique Postcards

201

*We live but once
To hell with the Diet*

*Say! What's th' matter with ya kid
Are ya' handcuffed?*

On the job

American postcard illustrator, Charles R. Twelvetrees worked for Alpha Publications, S. Bergman, Edward Gross, Illustrated Postal Card, National Art Company, Reinthal & Newman, F.A. Stokes, Raphael Tuck, and Ullman.

Little is known of his life. He died April 7, 1948 in the Hotel Le Marquis in New York, New York. §

*If you must have a BIRTHDAY
have a happy one.*

*Does anybody know where there's
a big Ice Cream Soda what wants
a Good Home?*

*If she won't kiss me
I'll spill the boat*

202

More young people attend college now than dreamed possible at the turn of the century. Like the students of today, there was great interest in souvenirs of their schools.

Postcards, featuring images or symbols of institutions of higher learning from the early 1900s, are highly collected.

These cards were generally published in sets of six and featured Eastern colleges. Tuck 2514 features Wesleyan, Dartmouth, Bowdin, Amherst, Brown and Williams. Tuck 2625 is illustrated. F. Earl Christy designed many university girls postcards. §

Raphael Tuck Series 2625

Harvard

Cornell

Pennsylvania

Princeton

Columbia

Yale

Louis Wain, an English artist, created hundreds of illustrations featuring cats. His major production period was from 1890 to 1914. Wain illustrated books and magazines, postcards, gift enclosure cards, and created pottery. He started his career drawing other animals, though cats were his first love and later became his lasting trademark.

Born in England in 1860, Wain was the only son in a family of six children. In 1879, Wain's father became ill with cirrhosis of the liver from chronic jaundice and was unable to work. The family lived on his father's savings until Louis finished his classes at the West London School of Art and started to teach.

When Louis Wain was 20, his father died, leaving him the sole support for his mother and five sisters.

Wain was not a successful teacher. He was shy and felt, "that imparting knowledge to others he was not gaining knowledge himself."

One day while directed by a vision, he quit work and left home. It didn't last for long. He managed to get a small room with a table and chair. When sleeping became impossible, he returned home, using the small rented room for work during the day.

At the Wain home, Emily Marie Richardson was a nanny for Wain's youngest sister. Richardson and Wain fell in love and, despite her being ten years older, they married on January 30, 1884. Emily died three years later, after a long illness.

In 1881 the *Illustrated Sporting and Dramatic News* published Wain's first signed illustration of bullfinches, mistitled *Robins Breakfast*. Between 1895 and 1905 Wain produced illustrations for over 40 books. In 1907, he drew comic strips, *Cats About Town* and *Grimalkin*, for the American syndicate of William Hearst's newspapers. His intended four month stay stretched into more than two years.

Wain suffered from terrible nightmares as a child. He wrote: "I seemed to live hundreds of years, and to see thousands of mental pictures of extraordinary complexity... But above all, I was haunted; in the streets, at home, by day and night, by a vast globe, which seemed to have endless surface, and I seemed to see myself climbing over and over it, until, from sheer fright I came to myself, and the vision went."

Louis Wain also recalled "At the age of six I dragged my little sister through a wilderness of streets to 'find the sea full of big ships', the vision of which is still with me."

As a child he rarely attended school, absent sometimes for months on end, commenting he could teach himself what was in libraries and school couldn't teach you the unknown. So why go?

Psychology textbooks reported that Louis Wain had schizophrenia. His art work has enabled scientific study of the progression of the disease.

In the beginning of Wain's career, his art work was more realistic. As the disease progressed, his work became more and more agitated. The wild expressions in his cat's eyes that stare with hostility reflect this agitation.

A psychotic often feels that a threatening world is staring at him. After some years, his disease progressed to the point where his cats became very hard to identify. The illustrations resembled the appearance of wall paper designs.

While Wain was very successful as an artist, he was an extremely poor manager of money. He received great commissions, which would practically disappear before his eyes. He was a soft touch for any request concerning donations to cat organizations.

These characteristics can be related to schizophrenia. The patient's intelligence may seem normal, but his emotions are very child-like. In schizophrenia, the person may isolate himself from others and his emotions slowly diminish. These patients often suffer from hallucinations or ideas of being persecuted.

During the end of his career, his mind failed completely and he was admitted to a mental hospital. After a few years, Dan Rider discovered Wain on a visit to the institution and drew his plight to the attention of the public. A few people, lead by Mrs. Cecil Chesterton, established a fund to transfer him to a more comfortable private institution. There he spent the last fifteen years of his life. He died in 1939.

During the entire postcard era, he produced designs for over 600 postcards, published by over 80 different publishers, such as Collins, Davidson, Davis, Dutton, Alpha, and Valentine.

His cats reflected the social history of the time and, more often than not, behaved as young adults, not children. A good example is his Charlie Chaplin series. Among the most sought after are his cats dressed as Santa Claus, the advertising postcards for his annuals, and the postcard paper dolls.

CHARLIE HAS A GREAT NIGHT OUT, FEELING SATISFIED, NO DOUBT

CHARLIE SAUNTERS BY THE TIDE, WITH HIS SWEETHEART BY HIS SIDE

WHEN CHARLIE GOES ON A WALK EACH DAY HE CARRIES HIS DOG IN HIS OWN FUNNY WAY

This colorful Tuck Oilette, series 3385, is titled, *Dressing Dolls' Fairy Tales, Series Five.* The six cards include: *Cinderella*; *Robinhood*; *Little Red-Riding Hood*; *Beauty and the Beast*; *Alladin*; *The Princess and the Magician*; and *Dick Whittington*.

For reasons unknown, the *Dick Whittington* card is the rarest in this already scarce set. Wain signed all cards, except for *Robinhood*.

There are several reasons for the scarcity of paper doll postcards. First, they were designed to be toys for children.

The instruction on the back of the postcard is, "Carefully cut the cat out with a pair of scissors..." Second, they were produced late in the postcard era, when public interest for postcard collecting was starting to decline, therefore, fewer were printed. §

Bernhardt Wall was born in Buffalo on December 30, 1872 and died in Los Angeles on February 9, 1956.

Wall's first job was with Ullman, who had hired him to create illustrations for their frames to increase sales. When a postcard company stole Wall's designs, Ullman changed from frame production to postcards. Wall's *Sunbonnet girls* were a great success, as were *Little Breeches*. These cards, numbered Ullman 1871-1876, were expanded later in a 2000 number series.

Cards designed by Wall were published by Valentine & Sons, Bergman, Barton and Spooner, International Art Co., the Illustrated Postal Card Co., Gibson Art Co., and J.I. Austen. More than fifteen publishers issued his cards. §

1871

1872

1873

1874

1875

1876

TSN 1895

Ida Waugh's work is often confused with the early work of Frances Brundage or Maude Humphrey.

While these postcards are not signed, series TSN 1895 was taken directly from the book, *When Mother was a Little Girl*, illustrated by Ida Waugh with verses by Amy E. Blanchard and others. Published by Ernest Nister of London and E.P. Dutton & Company of New York, the book contains 33 beautiful color images. Theo. Stroefer of Nuremberg (TSN), Germany, published these cards. §

Baby May

When Mother was a Little Girl

What the "Tick, Tick" says

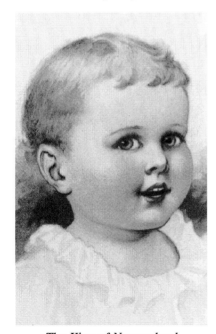

The King of Nurseryland

Hide and Seek

Where is Baby?

Walter Wellman was born in New Hampshire on May 25, 1879. During his college years, he studied architecture at Massachusetts Institute of Technology, and was the art editor for the college newspaper.

At school, he published a college calendar, resulting in free-lance work for the *Boston Globe* creating picture puzzles and comics. Though Wellman completed his degree in 1902, he decided to go to New York, New York, and start a career in comic art, instead of architecture.

Wellman's work was published by *Harper's*, *Judge*, *Women's Home Companion*, *Life* and *Puck*. In addition, he produced a weekly Sunday children's puzzle for the *New York Tribune*.

Wellman's first postcard copyrights appeared in 1906 on cards he published himself and sold through his New York office. There are a few examples which Rose Publishing Company did in 1906, but most of Wellman's work was self published.

This calendar set is from his first year at work and probably was created due to his success in college producing calendars. The copyright was filed November 30, 1906. Each heart vignette features a motif to reflect the month of the year. These cards are: *The Introduction* (January), *How Easy* (February), *The Naughty Wind* (March), *April Showers bring forth Rubbernecks* (April), *Paddling Her Own Canoe* (May), *The June Bride* (June), *Going Up* (July), *Going Down* (August), *When the Heart is Full of Girls* (September), *Carrying Her Grip* (October), *Her Thanksgiving Dinner* (November), and *Under the Mistletoe* (December).

Each card used the same green leaf pattern behind the heart motif. A touch of red inking was used somewhere within each heart. Using a minimum amount of color and changing only the calendar pages and interior heart motifs, Wellman reduced production costs. Because it was a calendar, buyers were forced to purchase twelve postcards. This series is rare. Perhaps due to his late copyright date, the material was hard to sell to shops or jobbers as most calendars are sold early in September or October. This could account for so few being available in today's market.

The postcard business was profitable enough for Wellman that, in 1909, he incorporated his business as the Walter Wellman Company, Inc. However, his last postcard designs were copyrighted on September 28, 1910. By 1917, he was working in New Jersey as a secretary, doing only a few free-lance puzzles and crosswords for magazines.

He married Matilda Richey in 1905. She died in 1945. Wellman remarried Martha Lucie, but died shortly after that of a stroke at the age of 70 on October 14, 1949.

Many of Wellman's cards are collected today, such as sets: *Need a Doctor?* (1908), *Merry Widow Wiles* (1908), *Last Will and Testament* (1908), *Weaker Sex* (1908), *Hand Series* (1908), *The Suffragette* (1909) and *Life's Little Tragedies, in Three Acts* (1909).

The calendar and Suffragette series are the most desirable to own. §

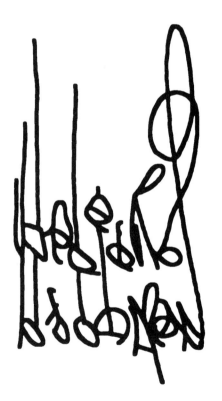

Walter Wellman's Signature

—— Rare Calendar Set ——

The Introduction

How Easy

The Naughty Wind

April Showers...

Paddling Her Own Canoe

The June Bride

Going Up

Going Down

When The Heart is Full...

Carrying Her Grip

Her Thanksgiving Dinner

Under The Mistletoe

The Austro-Hungarian Empire of Emperor Franz Josef was one of the great powers of Europe during the last half of the 19th century. It encompassed Hungary, Czechoslovakia, parts of Yugoslavia, Poland, Rumania, Russia and Italy. Vienna was the imperial capital. Postcards were issued for the first time in Austria and the quality of the design and craftsmanship of this country was never exceeded.

Many important publishers were located in Vienna, such as M. Munk, Philipp & Kramer, Gerlach & Schenk and Wiener Werkstaette. The most important artists, relating to art nouveau and the Secession school of art, were located in Austria. They used the picture postcard to get their work to the eyes of the public.

In 1903, Josef Hoffmann and Kolomon Moser founded the Wiener Werkstaette, an arts and crafts cooperative that created stylish furniture, fashions, carpets, wallpapers, silverware, glassware and postcards. Industrialist Fritz Waerndorfer funded the cooperative.

The workshop adopted a high standard of design based on the theory that, if everyday things were things of beauty, people would lead less suffocating lives. In 1905, the Wiener Werkstaette published its goals as "to establish intimate contact between public, designer and craftsman, and to produce good, simple domestic requi-

sites... to decorate, but without compulsion to do so, and certainly not at any cost... So long as our cities, our houses, our rooms, our furniture, our effects, our clothes and our jewelry, so long as our language and our feelings fail to reflect the spirit of our times in a plain, simple, and beautiful way, we shall lag infinitely far behind our ancestors."

This Vienna workshop broke with the Secessionist curvilinear style, but kept its decorative ideals. The Wiener Werkstaette worked beyond curves into bold geometry.

Emil Hoppe, a student of Hoffmann, designed the first four postcards produced by the Wiener Werkstaette, or Vienna Workshop, for the Kunstschau or emperor's jubilee celebration. The unnumbered cards of the Wiener Werkstaette were for specific events. The numbered series started in 1908 and continued until World War I with over 1,000 designs created. Some designs were artist signed, but rarely dated.

The quality of these cards is, without question, the best. Graphic designers from the entire region participated; Hungarians: Diveky and Pranke, Bohemians: Alber, Janke, Wenzel and Teschner, Moravians: Jung and Schwetz, Germans: Jesser and Jungnickel, and Russians: Makowska and Luksch.

Forty eight different artists designed the over 1,000 post-

card series. These artists varied greatly in age, resulting in a variety of styles. The geometric style of Hoppe and Kalhammer, the expressionist style of Kokoschka, Shiele, Jung and Kalvach and the fantasy style of Diveky, Wimmer, Lendecke and Likarz were represented by this series of postcards.

The postcards were a means of financial support for the other activities of the Wiener Werkstaette. They were involved with all aspects of fashion, from designs to fabrics and accessories. The Wiener Werkstaette dictated the style until 1920. These postcards played an important role in advertising the work of the Viennese workshop.

The Wiener Werkstaette postcards are not uniform in size. Some are very large, some oblong, some square, and some standard proportions. They have very distinctive postcard backs (see illustration).

The postcards, illustrated here, are three very different styles by three of the Wiener Werkstaette artists. While none of these cards are inexpensive, the designs illustrated are among the most expensive. The postcards, featuring the views of buildings or wallpaper type designs with Jewish New Year greetings in the center, are the least collected. The postcard designs, featuring fashions with little detail, are easier to find than the type illustrated. §

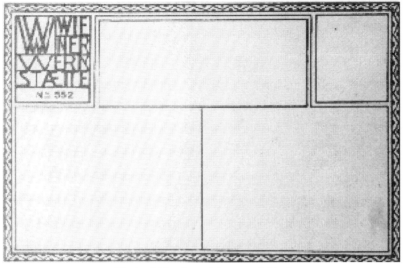

Typical Numbered Postcard Back

Diveky   *Kokoschka*   *E.T.*

WINSCH

John O. Winsch, of Stapleton, New York, was a publisher of superior quality greeting postcards.

He first issued postcards in 1910, shortly after the passage of the Payne-Aldrich Act, which increased tariffs on imported cards. The Winsch cards were printed in Germany and imported into the United States for distribution.

Winsch postcards sold at two for five cents, when the common price was one cent each. While some Winsch postcards were issued in sets of six; most of the better designs were issued in sets of four.

The most collected of the Winsch postcards are the Halloween designs by American art nouveau artist, Samuel L. Schmucker.

Winsch reached its peak in 1911, but continued in business until 1915. During this short time Winsch copyrighted over 3,000 designs.

This set is from 1910. §

My Hat Is Still In The Ring (Roosevelt)

Every time I come to town... (Champ Clark)

Wire tails were a clever novelty created by the postcard industry to enhance sales of fairly mundane subject matter.

Most are metallic in color, but occasionally cards feature a painted wire tail, like the white enameled tail on the mouse.

The tails are fine, tightly coiled wire with a springy action. Coupled with the illustration, they often give the animal the appearance of running.

While very few of these cards are expensive, there is always the exception to the rule. The political cards, featured here, are that exception.

Roosevelt did not run in 1908 and encouraged Taft to run. But, by 1912, he felt Taft was not a suitable President and sought his parties nomination, but lost it. Roosevelt ran on the Progressive Party ticket. His Bull Moose Party wire tail postcard is very desirable.

Eugene Chafin of Illinois ran in 1912 on the Prohibition ticket and Eugene Debs, as several times before, ran on the Socialist Party ticket.

Champ Clark, Speaker of the House, a Democratic party hopeful from Missouri, ran using the slogan, *Every time I come to town, The Boys start Kicking My Dog Aroun', Makes no difference if he is a houn', They gotta quit kicking my dog around*. The wiretail card for Clark is the hardest to find.

Wilson ultimately won the nomination after many ballots as a compromise between Champ Clark and Judson Harmon, Governor of Ohio. Wilson won the election because of vote splitting between Taft and Roosevelt.

The cards have survived well in terms of novelty cards. Usually the tails were secured between the front and back of the cards. Some publishers, however, poked the tails through the front of the cards and secured the tails with a white paper circle on the back. Glassine envelopes were used to mail both types of cards, protecting the hands of the letter carriers sorting mail. §

Has He Got Enough Steam? (Taft)

Will He Get Stung? (Wilson)

WOOD

Clarence Lawson Wood was born in 1878 in England. He lived and worked in Sussex County, Southern England.

He was one of the greatest illustrators of humor in Europe. A leading poster designer at that time, Ludwig Holwein of Munich, Germany, said,

"Lawson Wood is not only a great artist, painter and illustrator, but he is a delineator of type, character and humor unexcelled."

Collier's, a national weekly publication, launched Wood's career in the United States with magazine covers featuring his

lovable monkey family. *Collier's* wrote, "the first cover design was so original thousands of people immediately wrote for extra prints."

The antics of the monkeys graced magazines, postcards, blotters, advertising premiums and thrust the monkey into

Smoking cabbage

What? -- again!

GP -- Belives in being air-minded

Raising the wind

With lots of luck

The finishing touch

WOOD

prominence as a viable character for stuffed toys.

Gran'pop was a central character of many designs. The grandchildren always gave him grief when left in his charge. Wood's characters included parrots and pigs but the monkey was his trademark.

Wood's work was published by D. Allen, Brown and Bigelow, Carlton, Davidson, E. J. Hey, J. Henderson, S. Hildesheimer, International Art, Salmon Brothers, A. Stiebel, Tuck and Valentine.

He continued to produce work until his death in 1957. §

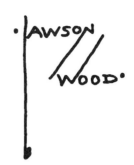

Jump to it!

Gran'pop likes being chiropped

Gran'pop's shadow show

Persuasion is better than force

Gran'pop invents a submarine

Step on it, Horace!

Pioneer Die Cut Postcard by Otis F. Wood

Livermore and Knight Company

Calendar Cards 1912

R.F. Outcault Copyright 1910

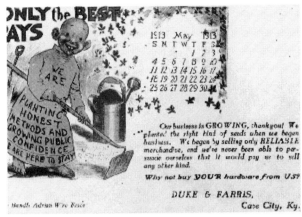

Calendar Cards From 1913 - 1915

Clare Victor Dwiggins

Mitchell Months of the Year
by AENZ

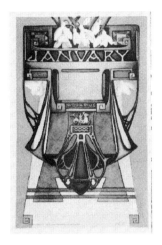

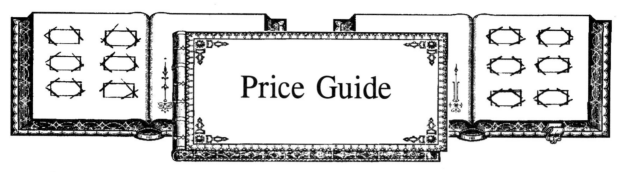

Price Guide

This guide contains prices of illustrated cards, marked with an asterisk (*), plus many that are not illustrated. All (see Reference) entries refer to other catagories within the price guide.

TITLE PAGE

*My favorite postcard (Frog)	$3-6

INTRODUCTION

*Name-Couth Souvenir, set	$200-250
*Printed RFD wagon	$6-8
*Easter cards	$4-6
*Tuck competition card	$15-20

BEGINNERS

*Mail box, set	$60-85

WHY COLLECT

*Hobbies	$8-10
*Girl at desk	$6-8
*Real photo shop interior	$150-250
*Elephant	$20-25

BECOMING A DEALER

*French, set	$400-450

ATTWELL

*Early signed and unsigned Tuck	$15-25
*Valentine & Sons up to #5000	$12-20
Postcards for Enesco figurines	$25-35
Valentine & Sons #5000 and up	$8-12
With dolls	$15-18
With black cats	$12-15

AVIATION

*Tuck, each card	$10-12
Real photo, highest prices for named aviators & commercial carriers	

BACHRICH

*La Danse, each card	$25-35

BAKST

*Exhibition of the Secession	$125-225
*La Fee de Poupee's, each card	$90-125

BASCH

*Female warriors, each card	$200-300

BEARS

*Child with bear, each card	$8-10
*Complete set	$75-100
Roosevelt bears (1-16)	$20-30
Roosevelt bears (17-32)	$35-45
Roosevelt bears, unnumbered	$100-150
(see Cavally, Cracker Jack, Ellam, Denslow, Greiner, Installment)	

BERTIGLIA

*Political, each card	$15-25
Children	$10-15
Women	$20-25

PRICE GUIDE

BILLIARDS

*Tuck or JVA, each card	$6-10
*Complete set	$60-85

BILLIKENS

*Political, each card	$200-250
*Regular, any message	$6-10

BOILEAU

*KNG or Osborne	$150-300
Other than Reinthal & Newman	$45-95
Reinthal & Newman, under #900	$12-20
Reinthal & Newman 900 series	$45-65
Reinthal & Newman watercolor series	$35-55
Tuck Connoisseurs	$125-200

BOULANGER

*Humorous Cats, each card	$25-35
Large cats	$15-25
Rabbits	$10-15
Small cats	$10-15

BOY SCOUTS

*Our Boys Scouts, each card	$150-200
Mottoes	$10-15

BRILL

*Ginks, each card	$8-12

BROWNE

*Baseball, each card	$20-30

BRUNDAGE

*Little Sunbeam	$35-45
Early, undivided back, chromos	$35-55
Most cards	$15-20

BRUNELLESCHI

*Art Deco, each card	$100-150
Art Nouveau, each card	$200-300

BULL DURHAM

*Each card	$75-100
*Complete set	$2500-3000

BYRRH

*Kirchner	$350-500
Most cards	$85-150

CADY

*Quaddy, each card	$35-45
*Complete with envelope	$450-500

CAMPBELL'S KIDS

*Vertical (#1-24), each card	$125-175
*Suffrage message (#7)	$175-250
Horizontal (#1-4), each card	$35-45

CARR

*St. Patrick's, each card	$6-10
Card with marbles	$10-15
Most cards	$6-10

CAVALLY

*Mother Goose series, each card	$10-15

CHIOSTRI

*Women, each card	$20-45
Children	$15-20

CHRISTY

*Kings & Queens, each card	$65-85
*Williston	$100-150

PRICE GUIDE

CLAPSADDLE

*Pro-Suffrage	$65-85
*Anti-Suffrage	$25-35
*Mechanical Halloween, black child	$350-450
*Halloween, orange or black background, each card	$45-65
Children	$8-15
Crosses, sleds, floral	$2-3
Kaleidoscopes	$65-85
Mechanical Halloween, white children	$200-225

CLAY

*Women, each card	$35-55

CORBELLA

*Women, each card	$20-25

CORVA

*Roma, each card	$50-75

CRACKER JACK

*Bears, each card	$35-45
*Bears, #5, #12, #16, each card	$45-55

CRAMER

*Children, each card	$15-20
Santa Claus	$30-45

CRITE

*Political, each card	$15-25
*With golf club	$25-30
*With teddy bear	$35-45

DARLING

*Cartoons, each card	$15-20

DAYS OF THE WEEK

*Children, each card (see Sunbonnets)	$8-12

DENSLOW

*Bears 1 & 2, each card	$15-20
*Bears 3 & 4, each card	$45-55
*Thanksgiving, each card	$10-15

DRAYTON

*Stages of Life, each card	$35-45
*Halloween, each card	$85-125
Adam and Eve	$55-65
Blatz beer advertising	$85-100
Drayton look-a-likes	$6-10
General advertising	$65-85
Klever Kards (see Campbell's Kids)	$45-65

DUDOVICH

*Art Deco, each card	$25-45

DWIG

*Coates & Company, each card	$35-45
*Halloween, each card	$25-30
*Widow's Wisdom, each card	$85-100
Unsigned Tuck, set (see Zodiac)	$65-75

ELLAM

*Breakfast in bed, each card	$15-25
*Puzzle, each card	$35-45
Teddy bears	$20-25

EVOLUTION

*Afro-American	$65-95
*Irishman or Chinaman	$10-18
Others	$10-18

224

PRICE GUIDE

EXPOSITION

*Newark, each card	$55-75
*1900 Paris Exposition, Jumeau, each card	$100-150
*Pan Pacific, each card	$25-35
*Denmark Bldg., each card	$15-20
Alaska-Yukon Pacific	$6-10
California Mid-winter	$200-300
Cotton States	$150-225
Hudson-Fulton	$8-12
Jamestown (A & V)	$5-9
Lewis & Clark	$10-15
Panama Pacific, general	$6-10
Pan American, general	$10-15
South Carolina Interstate and West Indian Exposition	$125-175
St. Louis (1904), general	$12-18
Trans-Mississippi	$85-125
World Columbian pre-Officials	$125-175
World Columbian Officials	$20-30
(see Hold to Light)	

FELIX

*Cats, each card	$15-25

FISHER

*Stages of Life, each card	$15-20
*Kiss	$15-20
*Nedra	$85-125
European publishers	$20-30
Most cards	$15-25

FLOWER CHILDREN

*Months of the Year, each card	$20-25
Set without months, each card	$15-20

FREXIAS

*Halloween	$75-80
*Valentines, each card	$20-35
(see Winsch)	

FROGS

*Frog in Throat, over sized	$55-65
Chromo Frogs, non-advertising	$25-35
Frog in Throat, small size	$45-55
Rotograph printed frogs, non-advertising	$6-20
(see Installment)	

GASSAWAY

*Children, each card	$10-15
Most cards	$6-12

GOLLIWOGGS

*Silver background, each card	$15-20
Signed Uptons, each card	$35-45

GREINER

*Molly and Teddy, each card	$15-20
Most cards	$8-15

GRIGGS

*Suffrage	$85-95
*Holidays	$8-12
*Large heart series, white children	$10-15
*Large heart series, black children	$15-25

GROUND HOG DAY

*Henderson, each card	$150-200
Late cards	$10-15
Linen cards	$25-35

GUTMANN

*Most cards	$40-50

HALLOWEEN

*Winsch set, each card	$85-125
*Winsch set of 3, each card	$200-300

*More interesting Halloween $12-25
Common Halloween $6-12
Least expensive Winsch Halloween $45-55
(see Clapsaddle, Dwig, Drayton,
    Frexias)

HAYS

*Children, each card $20-25
Most cards $6-12

HOLD TO LIGHT

*Art Nouveau style, each card $100-150
*Uncle Sam Santas, each card $1500-2500
*Koehler, *Fighting the Flames* $1500-2000
*St. Louis (1904), Inside Inn $150-300
*Holidays & animals, each card $35-55
Common, churches, landscapes $10-20
Common transparencies $8-20
Koehler Publishing, most $35-55
Mailick Santa $200-300
Red Santa $85-125
Santa, other colors $150-250
St. Louis (1904), general $30-40
St. Louis (1904), over sized $100-200
Winter to summer transparencies $35-55
(see Kirchner, Pigs)

ICART

*Signed Icart, each card $85-125
*Signed Helli, each card $55-75

INDIANS

*Sleepy Eye, monument $35-40
*Sleepy Eye, chief $95-125
*Others Sleepy Eye $65-95
Commercial color, printed $8-12
Commercial, linens $3-12
Comic $1-4
Real photo, autographed $65-85
Real photo, studio $25-35
Real photo, Indian life $55-65

INSTALLMENT

*Vertical Santa $200-250
*Santa, single card $15-25
*African warrior $85-100
*Swan $125-165
*Teddy bear $125-150
*Frog $100-125
*Horse $40-55
*Dog $50-65
*Cat $150-200
*Santa head RARE
Comic $25-45

JORDAN

*Happifats, each card $60-100

KING

*Coke $500-650
*Women, each card $25-35
Coke, Motor Girl $650-900

KIRCHNER

*Sunbursts, each card $85-100
*Charm series, each card $100-150
*Santoy series, each card $65-95
*Santa $350-450
*HTL, each card $300-400
Most early period $150-200
Most middle period $85-100
Most late period $35-65
(see Byrrh)

KLEIN

*Most alphabet, each card $15-25
*Alphabet: U, V, W, X, Y, Z $35-50
Most floral $3-10

KOEHLER

*Women, each card $85-150

PRICE GUIDE

Weiner Werkstatte	$200-450

KRUSE

*Dolls, each card	$10-15

LABOR DAY

*Nash, each card	$65-100
Lounsbury set, each card	$250-350
Lounsbury, Our Latest Holiday	$350-450

LE MAIR

*Children, each card	$12-18

LEWIN

*Signed, each card	$12-18
Santa	$25-35

LEYENDECKER

*Chesterfield, each card	$100-150

MAUZAN

*Months of the Year, each card	$25-35
Most cards	$20-25

McCAY

*Little Nemo, each card	$25-35

McMANUS

*Bringing Up Father, each card	$35-55

MECHANICAL

*PFB Punch and Judy, each card	$85-125
*Political, each card	$200-300
*Santa turn dial	$300-400
Cut outs for fingers	$10-25
Calanders	$12-20

Children in moving arm	$35-45
Gate cards with Santa	$100-175
Gate cards without Santa	$65-85
Girls popping out of bottles, cheese dishes, etc.	$125-165
Livermore & Knights	$20-85
Revolving snow window	$65-100
Turn wheel, change faces	$45-85
(see Clapsaddle)	

MICKEY MOUSE

*Mickey, each card, pre 1939	$25-35
Cards after 1940	$15-20
Cards after 1950	$8-10

MUCHA

*Months of year, each	$125-200
*Waverley, last sold for	$13,500
Early cards	$200-400
Slavic period	$65-100
Price guide to Mucha, see Martin in Sources	

O'NEILL

*Ice cream	RARE
*Birth announcement	RARE
*Pickings from Puck	$85-150
*Kewpie Klever Kards	$60-75
*Suffrage Klever Kard	$150-200
*Gross Kewpies	$100-125
Kewpies, Gibson	$35-45
Miniature Klever Kards	$85-100
Suffrage, Spirit of '76	$200-300
Suffrage, four babies	$450-500
Price guide to the postcards of Rose O'Neill, see Sources	

OPPER

*Comic, each card	$8-15
*Happy Hooligan	$10-12
Transformations	$6-8

PRICE GUIDE

OSTHAUS

*DuPont dogs, each card	$95-150
DuPont birds, each card	$35-50

OUTCAULT

*Bloomingdale's, each card	$85-125
Greetings	$10-15
Rockford Watch	$25-35
(see Yellow Kid)	

PAPER TOYS

*Milton, set	$600-800
*Peter Pan, set	$600-800
*Mack, set	$900-1200
*Mack, Golliwogg	$300-350
*Boxed, set	$1200-1500
*Fletcher books, each	$1000-1500

PHOTO

*Studio, each card	$5-8
*Merchant wagon	$150-250
*Interiors	$35-55
*Phonograph	$150-200
RFD wagons	$85-150
(see Introduction)	
Price guide to real photo, see Ward in Bibliography	

PIGS

*To Market, each card	$12-18
Chromolitho	$25-35
Dressed	$10-25
Hold to Light	$55-75
(see Thiele)	

POLITICAL

*Roosevelt, each card	$25-35
(see Bertiglia, Billikins, Crite Mechanical, Wire Tails)	

REISS

*Indians, each card	$18-25

ROCKWELL

*Advertising, each card	$35-65
*Nassau Tavern	$65-85

SCHMUCKER

*Letters From Home, each card	$75-100
*Mottoes, each card	$250-350
*Childhood Days, each card	$250-350
Winsch silk inserts	$65-85
Winsch full silks	$85-100
(see Halloween)	

SMITH

*Child in Garden, each card	$15-20

STATE GIRLS

*Puzzle with envelope	$35-55
*Plain	$15-20
Plain without state name	$17-22
Silk applied	$35-55

STOCK MARKET

*Each card	$15-25

STUDDY

*Bonzo, each card	$10-15
Bonzo with glass eyes	$25-35
Bonzo, not by Studdy	$8-12

SUFFRAGE

*Dunston-Weiler, each card	$25-35
*Ellam, each card	$35-45
(see Campbell's Kids, Clapsaddle, Griggs, O'Neill, Wellman)	

PRICE GUIDE

SUNBONNETS

*Days of the Week, each card	$12-18
Corbett	$15-25
Days of week	$10-15
Months of year	$10-15
Wall	$12-20

THIELE

*Cats, each card	$25-35
*Pigs, each card	$20-25
*Blacks, each card	$35-40
Cats, small images	$15-25

TWELVETREES

*Each card	$6-10

UNIVERSITY GIRLS

*Each card	$15-20

WAIN

*Cat Santas, each card	$200-300
*Charlie Chaplin	$200-300
*Paper dolls, each card	$250-350
*Dick Wittington	$400-450
Most cards	$35-50

WALL

*Little Breeches, each card	$8-12
Most cards	$6-10

WAUGH

*Children, each card	$30-40

WELLMAN

*Calendar, set	$150-250
Most cards	$8-12
Suffrage	$30-45

WIENER WERKSTAETTE

*Most cards	$100-300
*Top price	$2000-3000
Minimum	$35-45

Prices vary greatly, see French Neudin
    in Bibliography

WINSCH

*Children, each card	$40-45
*With Golly or Teddy	$45-55
Authors	$6-10
Common Holidays	$1-3
Halloween by Frexias	$65-125
New Year's Day by Schmucker	$50-75
Silk inserts	$3-10
St. Patrick's Day by Schmucker	$15-20
Valentine's Day by Frexias	$30-45
(see Halloween)	

WIRE TAILS

*Political, each card	$100-150
Most cards	$6-18

WOOD

*Most cards	$8-10
Pigs	$10-12

YELLOW KID

*Pioneer Yellow Kid	$1000-1500
*Livermore & Knight	$2000-2500
*Calendar, each card	$85-125
Buster Brown & His Bubble, each card	$35-55

ZODIAC

*Dwig, set	$150-200
*Mitchell without text, set	$120-150
Mitchell with text, set	$150-200
Colorful	$8-12
Plain	$4-6

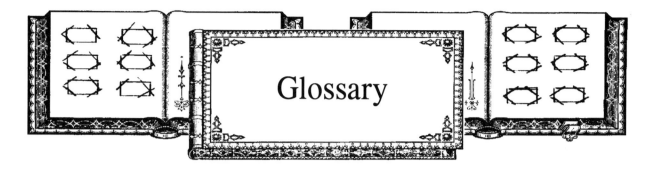

Glossary

Air Brush: An air brush applies a spray of paint, under compression, to a postcard that is usually embossed. The air brush technique allows for blended overlapping of colors and for a rapid application of color replacing time consuming hand painting.

Album Marks: Discoloration or heavy indentations on the corners of cards from the acid, leaching out of the antique album pages, or from weight.

Annual: A publication that appears every year. At the turn of the century, publishers produced these books for artists, such as Louis Wain and Mable Lucie Attwell, featuring the best of their work. Now, the Annual refers to a guide published each year by *The Postcard Collector*, listing all postcard clubs, postcard dealers and postcard shops, with articles about postcards.

Approval Service: A service whereby dealers send collectors postcards or photocopies of postcards priced for approval. The collector is under no obligation to buy and can return any or all items. Dealers establish who is responsible for the postage. A response should be made within ten days.

Arcade Cards: These items are postcard size, but with plain backs. They usually featured pin-up art and were sold in penny arcade vending machines.

Archival: Any museum quality material that will protect postcards for extended periods of time.

Artists: In Europe, this refers to cards of actors and actresses. In America, it refers to illustrators.

Artist Signed: Any postcard that has a printed signature of the illustrator. This does not mean that the postcard artist autographed the card, although examples of this do exist. If the publisher has printed a byline clearly identifing who did the work, the card is considered artist signed.

Checklist: A list composed by collectors to identify postcards designed by a certain artist or publisher. There are complete checklists of O'Neill, Brundage, Clappsaddle and Paul Finkenrath postcards (see Sources). It may refer to a list which collectors carry to identify cards needed to complete a certain set or series.

Chrome: Any card after 1939 with a shiny paper surface. The term is derived from Kodachrome.

Chromo Lithography: Color lithography, see lithography.

GLOSSARY

Condition: Refers to the physical condition of a postcard. Terms used are Mint, Near Mint, Excellent, Very Good, Good, Fair and Poor. Each dealer and auction house uses their criteria for assigning these terms. For example, some would call a card mint if used, but the card is in pristine condition; others would never refer to a used postcard as mint. It is best to understand the grading standards of each establishment.

Copper Windows: Flat printed view cards with copper metallic paint applied to the windows of the buildings. The results simulate Hold To Lights.

Copyright: The exclusive legal right of an author or artist or his agent to reproduce, publish, or sell a literary or artistic work.

Deeks: Postcard puzzles that change from one view to another simply by tilting the picture. This is sometimes achieved with a small paper tab across the bottom of the postcard.

Deltiology: Deltiology is the study of postcards; the person doing the research, a deltiologist. Randall Rhoades of Ashland, Ohio, first used the term. It means (from the Greek) the science or study (logos) of small pictures or cards (deltion).

Die Cut: Any paper object cut by the publisher into a shape other than a rectangle, such as the shape of an angel, Santa or animal.

Die Cut Hold to Light: A hold to light postcard that transforms from day to night when a bright light shows through the tiny holes cut on the surface of the card.

Distributor: A middle man who obtains the postcards wholesale and resells them. He may even be a wholesale distributor that sells them to shop owners. He does not create the design or pay for the printing of the cards.

Divided Back: A postcard back with a center line to divide the address from the message. Divided backs appeared in 1902 in England, 1904 in France, 1905 in Germany, and 1907 in the United States. This helps to date unused postcards. Cards before these dates have undivided backs.

D.R.G.M.: (Deutsches Reichsgebrauchmuster) German for *Design Registered* (not a publisher).

Embossed: Postcards that have designs slightly raised above the card's surface. Heavily embossed postcards have almost a papier-mache style, that stands greatly above the paper's surface.

Ephemera: Any printed or hand written item normally discarded after its intended use such as calendars, postcards, tradecards, and valentines.

Foxing: Brown spots in the paper's surface. These spots of mildew, penetrating the paper, cannot be removed by erasing but may occasionally be removed with bleaching.

Gelatin: A card with a varnish-like coating producing a glossy surface. The surface usually cracks or shatters. E.A.S. published the only gels guaranteed for life and they have lasted.

Golden Age of Postcards: From 1898 to 1918.

Government Postal: A postcard that has a preprinted stamp on the back. The government postal office issues these postcards and publishers use them to print designs and advertising messages. They were especially used before the Act of Congress 1898.

Gruss Aus: German for *Greetings From.*

Hold to Light: Any postcard that creates a different image if held to the light. Some are as simple as day into night, others as complicated as Winter into Summer. There are die cut hold to lights and transparencies.

Installment: A series of postcards designed to be sent one a day. The completed set forms one picture. Some installments are vertical pictures, such as an Uncle Sam figure; others form horizontal images, such as a running horse.

Linen: Postcards published in the late 20s through 50s, using a textured paper with a cross hatched surface. The surface resembles linen fabric. The cards romanticized the images of gas stations, diners, hotels and other commercial buildings. Using the photographic image of an establishment, all undesirable features, such as telephone poles, junk yards, background clutter, and sometimes even cars and people were removed by air brushing.

Lithography: A printing process using a smooth, flat, porous surface of stone on which the design is laid down with grease and water so that only certain parts will take the ink and print.

Mechanical: Postcards that have moving parts. It may be as simple as a die cut top revealing a different idea of the previous image when opened. It could as complicated as pulling a tab for a curtain to move and totally change pictures. Some mechanicals have wheels that change the faces on a body or dates on a calendar.

Mail Auction: A process of selling postcards through the mail by dealers or collectors. These may be privately printed auctions or ones that appear in the trade papers, such as *Barr's Postcard News* or *The Postcard Collector*. All bidding must be completed by the closing date. Each auction house has rules, which must be understood before bidding.

Mail Order: See approval service.

Miniature: Postcards done as a novelty during the Golden Age. They are about one half the size of the standard 3½ by 5½ inch postcards. They have stamp boxes and are often postally used. The most desirable are those by the Scandinavian artists or publisher John Winsch.

Net Price Sale: Sales usually conducted by mail or in the trade publications. Fixed prices are published for each item listed. The postcards are sold on a first come, first served basis.

GLOSSARY

Novelty: These cards include mechanicals, and cards that have items attached, such as bags of salt, real hair, metal medallions, paper applique, silk, or even pennies. Some novelty cards are die cut shapes or have holes in which fingers can be inserted to making the postcard figure appear to have real arms, legs, or even a nose.

Oilette: A term used by Raphael Tuck and Sons of England to refer to a particular style of postcard production. The oilettes often looked like oil paintings, with noticeable brush strokes.

Over Sized: The standard postcard size during the Golden Age was 3½ by 5½ inches; the standard modern postcard size is 4 by 6 inches. Any card larger than these sizes is considered oversized. Modern postcards are often called Continentals.

PVC: Poly vinyl chloride, polymers derived from vinyl chloride used to make plastic pages and sleeves. These can cause damage to postcards over time.

Pioneers: Postcards issued before the Act of Congress in 1898. They carry instructions on the back, such as, *Write the address only on this side - the message on the other*, or *Nothing but address can be placed on this side*, or *This side for address only*.

Postcard: A card specifically made with the intention that it could be used by itself as a mailed message or souvenir.

Printer: A company or individual who physically makes postcards. It is usually not the designer of the artwork or the distributor of the postcards, yet, it may be the publisher.

Private Postal: Postcards produced, not by the government, but by private business or publishers.

Publisher: A company or individual who initiated and funded the production of a postcard. They may or may not be the printer of the card. Many postcards identify the publisher. The publisher identification may be accompanied by a copyright date. Other times it clearly states published by... Publishers can be identified by trademark logos, or even the style of the printed word postcard. There may be names of printers or distributors on the backs of cards. These should not be confused with the name of the publisher.

Puzzle Cards: A European term for installments. In America, it refers to hidden picture cards, jigsaw puzzle postcards, rebus cards, or anything that is a puzzle to solve.

Radiol: Postcards produced by Paul Finkenrath of Berlin (PFB). The cards have decorative highlights of applied metallic paint, usually copper colored.

Real Photo: A term coined to distinguish between commercially printed photographic images and an actual photograph printed on photograph paper with a preprinted postcard back. Real photo cards are more desirable than commercially printed postcards. Most real photos are one of a kind, while commercially printed photographs were produced in large quantity.

GLOSSARY

Rebus: A puzzle postcard on which words, phrases, or sentences are represented by pictures of objects and signs, the names of which, when sounded in sequence, afford the solution.

S.A.S.E.: Self addressed stamped envelope. All dealer inquiries should include a S.A.S.E.

Sepia: A dark brown color applied to photographs or other prints. Inky secretions of the cuttlefish produce this coloration.

Series: Groups of postcards that belong together in a collection. The individual cards may or may not have been printed at the same time. Examples are: Sunbonnets, Bonzo, and Mickey Mouse. More than just a common topic, a series has a common artist and publisher.

Sets: Postcards published in a group of four, six, seven, eight, or twelve. These were sold in packets or individually. Examples are: days of the week or months of the year.

Silk: Postcards where silk fabric is applied to the design, or the total image is printed on silk fabric, then attached to a postcard back. See Woven in Silk.

Stereoscope: An optical instrument with two lenses, through which photographs taken in pairs from slightly different angles appear to have solidarity and relief.

Topics: Postcards that are not views, but are of subjects such as baseball, kites, cats, and golf.

Tradecards: Advertising cards issued before 1900. Store keepers gave them away in products or with the purchase of a product. They were very popular before the postcard and were often times glued into large scrap books with other die cut scrap.

Trademark: Protected by law, a registered symbol or device used exclusively by a single merchant or manufacturer on his goods to distinguish them from the goods made and sold by others.

Transparency: A type of Hold to Light postcard that creates its transformation with many thin layers of paper. A total change in image is caused by strong light behind the postcard. There are no die cut holes in the surface to achieve this transformation.

Undivided Back: A postcard back without a dividing line to separate the message from the address. Undivided backs on postcards help date the cards (see divided back).

View Cards: Postcards that feature cities and places within cities, such as views of parks, main streets, depots, store fronts, bridges, and roads. They are not of topics such as Halloween, cats, or Clapsaddle.

Woven in Silk: These cards have the design carefully woven into the silk fabric like a tapestry. T. Stevens of Coventry, England, produced many.

Bibliography

READ THE BIBLIOGRAPHY AND THE BOOKS TOO!

Many times collectors ask me, "How do you know that? How did you learn so much about postcards?" I *buy* books, I own all of these, and I *read* them. "Knowledge is Power", so it is said. Go to the library armed with this list and have them search for the out of print books through inter-library loan systems. Don't be afraid to buy or study from foreign language books. With an inexpensive paper back foreign language dictionary, you will figure it out. If you love your hobby, learn about its history and the artists who created the cards. Research makes the hobby so much more interesting.

Alderson, F. *The Comic Postcard in England Life*. 1969. David and Charles, Devon, England. Out of print.

Allen & Hoverstadt. *The History of Printed Scraps*. 1983. 175p. ;ill. 108 pages of color featuring hundreds of die cuts, ISBN 0-904568-25-3: New Cavendish Books, London, England. Out of print. Understanding what went before helps in postcard research. This book is one of the best on manufacturers and artists of die cut scraps. It lists virtually all the known scrap printers and manufacturers.

Allmen, Diane. *The Official Price Guide to Postcards*. 1990. 302p. ;ill. 350 black & white and color, ISBN 0-876-37802-5: House of Collectibles, New York, NY. This guide lists many topics and views with prices. It is somewhat hard for beginners to use because it takes knowledge of what you are trying to look up. The index is incomplete in terms of cross references and listings. The prices are accurate except for those where decimals were typeset incorrectly. This has been corrected in later printings.

Anderson, Will. *New England Roadside Delights*. 1989. 192p. ;ill. 400 black & white and color. $22.95. Will Anderson, 7 Bramhall Terrace, Portland, ME 04103. Contains many types of ephemera including linen postcards. Not quite as exciting as Baeder's book but well worth the money.

Arrasich, Furio. *Catalogo Delle Cartoline Italiane*. (in Italian), 224p. ;ill. 500 black & white and color. La Cartolina, Rome, Italy. Features many great cards, art nouveau, topics, and views.

Aylesworth & Aylesworth. *Chicago; The Glamour Years (1919-1941)*. 1986. 192p. ;ill. 400 black & white and color, ISBN 0-8317-1254-6: Gallery Books, New York, NY.

Babb & Owen. *Bonzo; The Life and Work of George Studdy*. 1988. 128p. ;ill. 1000 black & white and color, ISBN 0-903685-23-X: $50.00. Richard Dennis, Somerset, England. A terrific book with every known Bonzo postcard illustrated in color! About 1,000 different cards plus illustrations of china, dolls, and other memorabilia.

BIBLIOGRAPHY

Baeder, John. *Gas, Food, and Lodging; A Postcard Odyssey, through the Great American Roadside*. 1982. 132p. ;ill. 500 black & white and color, ISBN 0-89659-308-8 (cloth): Abbeville Press, Inc., 505 Park Avenue, New York, NY 10022. Terrific book, great information and a delight to read.

Baeder, John. *Diners*. 1981. 144p. ;ill. 117, 50 in color, ISBN 0-8109-2078-6: Harry N. Abrams, New York, NY. Another must buy book for collectors interested in Diners.

Banneck, Janet A. *The Antique Postcards of Rose O'neill*. 1992. 100p. ;ill. 200 black & white, ISBN 1-882207-00-9: $27.95. Greater Chicago Productions, P.O. Box 595, Lisle, IL 60532.

Baudet, F. *Encyclopedie Internationale de la Carte Postale*. (in French), 1978. 352p. ;ill. 1800 black & white and color. Self published. Out of print. A great book featuring 207 pages of French views and 159 pages of topics on postcards. Prices in francs are out of date now but still help with whether a card is 50 cents or $50.

Beetles, Chris. *Mabel Lucie Attwell*. 1988. 120p. ;ill. 100 color, ISBN 1-85145-282-6: $35.00. Pavilion Books Ltd., London, England. Great biographical information. The illustrations are super.

Blair, Arthur. *Christmas Cards for the Collector*. 1986. 128p. ;ill. 200 black & white and color, ISBN 0-7134-5224-2: Batsford Ltd., London, England. Out of print. A great book for understanding the beginning of greeting cards. Illustrations from 1798-1982.

Bourgeron, Jean-Pierre. *Nude 1900*. 1980. 64p. ;ill. 60 black and white (sepia toned) full size postcards, ISBN 0-87100-169-1: Morgan Press, New York, NY. Short biography of nude photography.

Bowers & Budd. *Harrison Fisher*. 1984. 372p. ;ill. 400 black & white. Self published. Out of print. A very complete checklist, description and commentary on Fisher. A must book for Fisher collectors.

Bowers & Martin. *The Postcards of Alphonse Mucha*. 1980. 120p. ;ill. 200 black & white, ISBN 0-911572-18-X: Mary Martin, 4899 Pulaski Hwy., Perryville, MD 21903. A comprehensive listing of the postcards of Mucha, a much needed tool if collecting art nouveau, the rarity guide is still current.

Buday, George. *The History of the Christmas Card*. 1954. 304p. ;ill. 50 black & white and color. Spring Books, London, England. Out of print. This book turns up at flea markets and antique shows. It is a good reference on the beginning of the Christmas ephemera production.

Budd, Ellen H. *Frances Brundage Post Cards: An Illustrated Reference Guide*. 1990. 140p. ;ill. 950 black & white, $25.00. Ellen H. Budd, 6910 Tenderfoot Lane, Cincinnati, OH 45249. The most complete listing of this artist's work, a must have if you collect Brundage. No price guide.

Budd, Ellen H. *Ellen H. Clapsaddle Signed Post Cards: An Illustrated Reference Guide*. 1989. 200p. ;ill. 2300 black & white, $30.00. Ellen H. Budd, 6910 Tenderfoot Lane, Cincinnati, OH 45249. The most complete listing of this artist's work, a must have if you collect Clapsaddle. No price guide.

Burdick, J. R. *Pioneer Postcards*. 1957. 144p. :ill. 300 black & white. Nostalgia Press, New York, NY. Out of print. Occasionally available from Greater Chicago Productions, P.O. Box 595, Lisle, IL 60532. The best book on Pioneer postcards to date, it is being updated.

Byatt, Anthony. *Collecting Picture Postcards - An Introduction*. 1982. 96p. ;ill. 85 black & white,

236

BIBLIOGRAPHY

ISBN 0-9506212-1-8: Golden Age Postcard Books, England.

Canemaker, John. *Felix, the Twisted tale of the World's most famous Cat.* 1991. 174p. ;ill. 100 black & white and color, ISBN 0-679-41127-X: $30.00. Pantheon Books, a division of Random House, Inc., New York, NY. Great research and wonderful illustrations.

Carline, Richard. *Pictures in the Post.* 1959. 128p. ;ill. 300 black & white & color. Deltiologists of America, P.O. Box 8, Norwood, PA 19074. Out of print.

Carver, Sally S. *The American Postcard Guide to Tuck.* 1976. 76p. ;ill. 600 black & white. Carves Cards. Self published. Out of print. Very useful guide to the number of cards in Tuck sets. Shows many examples.

Chase, Ernest Dudley. *The Romance of Greeting Cards.* 1927. 253p. ;ill. few. University Press, Cambridge, MA. This books intro says, "An historical Account of the Origin, Evolution, and Development of the Christmas Card, Valentine and Other Forms of Engraved or Printed Greetings from the Earliest Days to Present time." Which because of the copyright date means 1927. Watch for these kinds of books, they contain valuable information.

Christie, Victor J. W. *Bessie Pease Gutmann.* 1986. 74p. ;ill. 12 black & white and color. Park Avenue Publishers, Ocean Township, NJ. Contact: Gutmann Collectors Club, Inc., P.O. Box 486, Neptune, NJ 07754. The 65 known postcards are listed with biographical information.

Cope, Peter & Dawn. *Illustrators of Postcards from the Nursery.* 1978. 64p. ;ill. 70 black & white and color, ISBN 0-904499-05-7: East West Publications, London, England. Biographies of 12 postcard illustrators, mostly English, but a nice reference.

Corson, Walter C. *Publisher's Trademarks Identified.* 1962. ISBN 0-913782-11-7: Deltiologists of America, P.O. Box 8, Norwood, PA 19074.

Dale, Rodney. *Catland.* 1977. 30p. ;ill. 14 8x10 color, ISBN 0-7156-1164-X: Duckworth & Co. Ltd., London, England. The text and great selection of Wain illustrations make this book a delight.

Dale, Rodney. *Louis Wain the Man who drew Cats.* 1968. 200p. ;ill. 300 black & white, ISBN 7183-0141-2: Fletcher & Son Ltd., Norwich, England. Out of print. If you love Wain postcards, find this book. The best written. No substitute.

Deguy, Michael (Introduction) Collection of Andreas Brown. *L'Amerique au fil des jours.* (in French) 1983. 70p. ;ill. 64 black & white (sepia toned), ISBN 2-86754-006-2: Centre National de la Photographie, Paris, France. This small book is a pure joy with full size illustrations of great real photo postcards of people in strange places or with strange props. Reflects the joy of collecting real photography.

Delulio & Ross. *Especially Cats: Louis Wain's Humorous Postcards.* 1985. 315p. ;ill. 900 black & white. Self published. This comprehensive guide to the postcards of Louis Wain is a must for Wain collectors. Clearly done, divided by publishers, well described.

Duval & Monahan. *Collecting Postcards; 1894-1914.* 1978. 212p. ;ill. 100 color, ISBN 0-7137-0823-9: Blandford press, Ltd., England.

Edwards & Ottaway. *The Vanished Splendor: Postcard Views of Early Oklahoma City.* 1982. 61p. ;ill. 185, all color, ISBN 0-910453-00-4: $19.95. Abalache Book Shop Publishing Co., 311 South Klein, Oklahoma City, OK 73108. A great book on Oklahoma City, a style worth studying if you intend to do any other city.

Edwards & Ottaway. *The Vanished Splendor II: A Postcard Album of Oklahoma City.* 1983. 88p. ;ill. 240, all color, ISBN 0-910453-01-2: $19.95. Abalache Book Shop Publishing Co.,

311 South Klein, Oklahoma City, OK 73108. The success of the first volume created a need for this. Great job.

Fanelli & Godoli. *Art Nouveau Postcards*. (in Italian) 1985, (in English) 1987. 370p. ;ill. 500 color, ISBN 0-8478-0832-7: $75.00 (hardbound). Rizzoli International Publishing, Inc., 597 Fifth Avenue, New York, NY 10017. This book first appeared in Italian, I bought it and struggled until the English version was issued. The best on the subject matter and well worth the price.

Feaver, William. *Masters of Caricature*. 1981. 240p. ;ill. 500 black & white and color. Alfred A. Knopf, New York, NY. A great research tool for understanding the caricature and humor of the turn of the century.

Ferrier, Jean-Louis (editor in chief). *Art of Our Century; The Chronicle of Western Art - 1900 to the Present*. 1988. 896p. ;ill. 900 black & white and color, ISBN 0-13-011644-0: Prentice Hall, New York, NY.

Forissier, Beatrix. *30 Annees d'elegance a travers la carte postale*. (Thirty Year History of Postcards 1900-1930) (in French), 1978. 190p. ;ill. 500 black & white, ISBN 2-85917-008-1: Wonderful illustrations, not much text.

Forissier, Beatrix. *25 ans d'actualities a travers La Carte Postale*. (Twenty Five Year History of Post Cards 1889-1914) (in French), 1976. 160p. ;ill. 300 black & white and color. Imprimerie Sitec, 8 Rue Milton, Paris, France 75009. Wonderful illustrations, not much text.

Fricke, Charles A. *A Contemporary Account of the First United States Postal Cards 1870-1875*. 1973. 146p. ;ill. 150 black & white. Self published. Out of Print. A very complete history of this time period.

Garnier & Lluch. *Cartes Postales d'illustrateurs*. (Postcard Illustrators; a Dictionary of Signatures and Monogrammes.) (in French), 1984. 290p. ISBN 2-905-29700-X: Societe d'Edition et de Diffusion Artistique, Laneuville Au Pont, 52100 Saint Dizier, Paris, France. A superb book of monograms and signatures. Helps identify those great European artists, being in French is no detriment.

Greenhouse, Bernard L. *Political Postcards; 1900-1980*. 1984. 109p. ;ill. 350 black & white. Postcard Press, Syracuse, NY 13217. Out of print. A great book to give the collector an idea of what is available, each election year represented, not comprehensive but the best to date.

Guptill, Arthur L. *Normal Rockwell Illustrator*. 1946. 208p. ;ill. 600 black & white and color. Watson-Guptill Publications, New York, NY.

Hansen, Traude. *Die Post Karten der Wiener Werkstatte*. 1982. 328p. ;ill. 1000 black & white, ISBN 3-923239-01-7: Verlag Schneider - Henn - Munchen - Paris.

Hill, C. W. *Discovering Picture Postcards*. 1970. 64p. ;ill. 37 black & white, ISBN 8563102-2: Shire Publications, England.

Hillier, Bevis. *Greetings from Christmas Past*. 1982. 95p. ;ill. 300 color, ISBN 0-906969-23-9: The Herbert Press Limited, London, England. Postcards and Trade cards used to illustrate the traditions of Christmas. Nicely done.

Holt, Toni and Valmai. *Picture postcards of the Golden Age : A Collector's Guide*. 1971. 214p. ;ill. 79 black & white and color. Deltiologists of America, P.O. Box 8, Norwood, PA 19074. Out of Print. Strong text, slanted towards English market.

Holt, Toni and Valerie. *Till the Boys Come Home; The Picture Postcards of the First World War.*

1977. 192p. ;ill. 900 black & white and color, ISBN 0-913782-08-4: Deltiologists of America, P.O. Box 8, Norwood, PA 19074. Informative book on the war with an English point of view.

Jaramillo, Alex. *Cracker Jack Prizes*. 1989. 96p. ;ill. 700 color, ISBN 1-55859-000-5: $19.95. Abbeville Press, New York, NY. Pictures all postcards in color.

Kaduck, John M. *Mail Memories*. 1971. Self published. Out of print. Great illustrations, no text, price guide completely out of date.

Kaduck, John M. *Rare and Expensive Postcards*. 1974. 86p. ;ill. 1000 black & white. Wallace Homestead, Des Moines, IA. Out of print. No text and many cards are neither rare or expensive but it shocked the postcard world with its high prices in 1974, now they seem cheap beyond belief. Does show interesting cards.

Kaduck, John M. *Rare and Expensive Book II*. 1979. 134p. ;ill. 1000 black & white and color. Wallace Homestead, Des Moines, IA. Out of print. Most cards from the collection of Ellen Budd, many rare and unusual cards illustrated. Again prices seemed high then but about 20 percent below market now.

Kana-Butrica, Mary Gail. *The Historical Paintings of Alfons Mucha: The Slav Epic*. 1979. 137p. ;ill. 59 black & white, THESIS, The Graduate School of the University of Texas at Austin. This information packed thesis should be read by every collector of Mucha. The author spent a great deal of time with Mucha's daughter and gives a different perspective than the books by Mucha's son.

Keetz, Frank. *Baseball Comic Postcards*. 1983. 59p. ;ill. 35 black and white. Keetz, 1426 Valencia Rd., Schenectady, NY 12309. This checklist is only artist illustrated, comic baseball postcards, but very well done.

Kery, Patricia Frantz. *Great Magazine Covers of the World*. 1982. 384p. ;ill. 500 color, ISBN 0-89659-225-1: $75.00. Abbeville Press, 488 Madison Avenue, New York, NY 10022. More than 500 great covers from 20 countries, spanning a century and a half of magazine publishing. The most fantastic book ever.

Kirsch, Chromos. *A Guide to Paper Collectibles*. 1981. 236p. ;ill. 100 black & white and color. A. S. Barnes & Co., Inc., New York, NY. Out of print. Great information on publishers and artists. A good reference book.

Klamkin, Marian. *Picture Postcards*. 1974. 192p. ;ill. nearly 700 black & white and color, ISBN 0-396-06889-8: Dodd, Mead & Company, New York. Out-of Print.

Kyrou, Ado. *L'Age D'Or de la Carte Postale*. (The Golden Age of the Postcard) (in French), 1966. 178p. ;ill. 600 black & white and color, ISBN 2-7158-0053-3: Andre Balland, Paris, France. Many categories of postcards illustrated of French topics and illustrators.

Laffin, John. *World War I in Postcards*. 1988. 201p. ;ill. 400 black & white and color, ISBN 0-86299-370-9: Alan Sutton, England. Every aspect of the Great War is depicted with postcard illustrations.

Latimer, Heather. *Louis Wain; King of the Cat Artists, A Dramatized Biography*. 1982. 166p. ;ill. 50 black & white, ISBN 0-943698-00-6 (hardcover): $50.00. Papyrus Publishers, P.O. Box 466, Yonkers, NY 10704. A great story but it must be remembered it is dramatized based on only some fact.

Lee, Ruth Webb. *A History of Valentines*. 1952. 239p. ;ill. 300 black & white and color, ISBN 0-910872-10-4: Lee Publications, MA. Out of print. For any one interested in valentines or valentine postcards. Here is information on artists, publishers, and symbols of the holiday. The best book, look for it.

Leler, Hazel. *Winsch Halloween Post Card Check List*. 1982. 26p. ;ill. 119 black & white. Leler, 12327 Windjammer. Houston, TX, 77072. Super list, new update being worked on now.

Leler, Hazel. *Stecher Halloween Post Card Checklist*. 1986. 21p. ;ill. 82 black & white. Leler, 12327 Windjammer, Houston, TX 77072. Great list, careful research.

Le Roque & Farago. *Disneyland-Walt Disney World Postcards; A complete checklist and Historical Guide*. 1979. 73p. ;ill. 5 black & white. R & N Postcard Company, P.O. Box 217, Temple City, CA 91780.

Le Roque & Farago. *L.H. "Dude" Larson Postcard Check List and Guide*. 1979. 40p. ;ill. 80 black & white. R & N Postcard Company, P.O. Box 217, Temple City, CA 91780.

Lesser, Robert. *A Celebration of Comic Art and Memorabilia*. 1975. 292p. ;ill. 500 black & white and color, ISBN 0-8015-1456-8: Hawthorn Books, Inc., 260 Madison Avenue, New York, NY 10016. Out of print. Great book about all types of comic illustrators. Super reference.

Lowe, James L. *Standard Postcard Catalog*. 1982. 288p. ;ill. 300 black & white, ISBN 0-913782-10-6: Deltiologists of America, P.O. Box 8, Norwood, PA 19074. Out of Print. Great listing of categories, but prices unreliable.

Lowe, James L. *Walden's Post Card Enthusiast Revisited*. 1982. 224p. ;ill. few, ISBN 0-913782-09-2: Deltiologists of America, P.O. Box 8, Norwood, PA 19074. This is a reprinting of the postcard newsletter by Orville C. Walden, New York, from 1950 to 1956.

Lyons, Forrest D., Jr. *The Artist Signed Postcard*. 1975. 88p. :ill. 800 black & white and color. L-W Promotions, Gas City, IN 46933. Out of print, pictures, no text.

Malton, Leonard. *Of Mice and Magic; A History of American Animated Cartoons*. 1980. 470p. ;ill. 200 black & white and color. McGraw-Hill Book Co., New York, NY. Out of print. A must find book for cartoon character postcards such as Mickey and Felix.

Margolies & Gwathmey. *Ticket to Paradise; American Movie Theaters and How we had Fun*. 1991. 144p. ;ill. 500 color, ISBN 0-8212-1829-8: $29.95. Little, Brown and Company, Boston, MA. Super book using many postcard images, but not about postcards.

Margolies, John. *The End of the Road*. 1981. 126p. ;ill. 150 color, ISBN 0-14-005840-0: Penguin Books, New York, NY. A good research book for what has existed along the highways of life over the last 7 decades. An American architectural heritage reference guide.

Mashburn, J. L. *The Postcard Price Guide*. 1992. 318p. ;ill. 300 black & white, ISBN 1-56664-009-1: $21.00. Colonial House, P.O. Box 609, Enka, NC 28728.

Mashburn, J. L. *The Super Rare Postcards of Harrison Fisher with price guide*. 1992. 68p. ;ill. 82 black & white, ISBN 1-56664-005-9: Colonial House, P.O. Box 609, Enka, NC 28728. This book is only about the Fisher cards published in Finland.

McAllister & Rinaberger. *Paul Finkenrath, Berlin (P.F.B.) Checklist*. 1990. 261p. ;ill. 56 black & white, $25.00. Rinaberger, 4548 Fairlane Dr. N.E., Cedar Rapids, IA 52402. A very complete listing, general price guide, no text but a great research tool for collectors of PFB.

McCanse, Ralph Alan. *Titans and Kewpies, the Life and Art of Rose O'Neill*. 1968. 220p. ;ill. 18 black & white. Vantage Press, Inc., New York, NY. Out of print. If you love Rose O'Neill, find this book. Out of print copies generally sell for $100-150.

McDonald, Ian. *Vindication! A Postcard History of the Women's Movement*. 1989. 127p. ;ill. 300 black & white and color, ISBN 0-947792-26-0: $30.00. Dierdre McDonald Books, Bellew Publishing Co., Ltd., 7 Southampton Place, London, England WC1A 2DR. A great book of the struggle for the right to vote. More than just a postcard book.

Megson Fred & Mary. *American Advertising Postcards; Sets and Series 1890-1920; A Catalog and Price Guide*. 1985. 329p. ;ill. over 2,000 black & white, $15.00. The Postcard Lovers, P.O. Box 482, Martinsville, NJ 08836. A scholarly book with index of products for ease of locating cards. Well worth owning.

Megson, Fred & Mary. *American Exposition Postcards 1870-1920; A Catalog and Price Guide*. 1992. 287p. ;ill. 2000 black & white, $20.00. The Postcard Lovers, P.O. Box 482, Martinsville, NJ 08836. A carefully researched work on expositions, prices reliable. Worth buying.

Miller, George & Dorothy. *Picture Postcards in the United States 1893-1918*. 1976. (see revised edition under Ryan) A must have book for serious collectors.

Monahan, Valerie. *An American Postcard Collector's Guide*. 1981. 128p. ;ill. 200 black & white and color, ISBN 0-7137-1113-2: $20.00. Blanford Press, England.

Mordente, Mario. *Catalogo delle Cartoline illustrate Italiane*. (in Italian or French), 1980. 245p. ;ill. 400 black & white and color. A & B, Rome, Italy. Features some of the wonderful Italian artists and advertising postcards.

Morgan & Brown. *Prairie Fires and Paper Moons; The American Photographic Postcard: 1900-1920*. 1981. 191p. ;ill. 300 black & white (sepia tones) full size, ISBN 0-87923-404-0: David R. Godine, Boston, MA. Out of print. This fantastic book set the postcard world on fire. It teaches what is available and its importance to the social history of this country. If you collect real photo postcards, find this book.

Mucha, Jeri. *Alphonse Maria Mucha*. 1989. 300p. ;ill. 250 color, ISBN 0-8478-1019-4: Rizzoli, New York., NY. A great book about the life and times of Mucha written by his son. The illustrations alone are well worth the price of the book.

Mucha, Henderson, & Scharf. *Mucha*. 1971, 1974. 144p. ;ill. 45 color, 100 black & white, ISBN 85676-102-5: St. Martin's Press, New York, NY. A biography of his life and art.

Muncaster & Yanow. *The Cat Made Me Buy It!* 1984. 96p. ;ill. 116 color, ISBN 0-517-55338-4: $7.95. Crown Publishing, New York, NY.

Muncaster & Yanow. *The Cat Sold It!* 1986. 96p. ;ill. 113 color, ISBN 0-517-56303-7: $9.95. Crown Publishing, New York, NY.

Muncaster & Sawyer. *The Dog Made Me Buy It!* 96p. ;ill. 130 color, ISBN 0-517-57453-5: $12.95. Crown Publishing, New York, NY.

Muncaster, Sawyer & Kapson. *The Baby Made Me Buy It!* 96p. ;ill. 120 color, ISBN 0-517-58206-6: $14.00. Crown Publishing, New York, NY. All four of the Muncaster books show great care in research and selection of illustrations. Postcards are included and all items are in color. Great value.

Musser, Cynthia Erfurt. *Precious Paper Dolls*. 1985. 238p. ;ill. 500 black & white and color, ISBN:0-87588-254-4: $14.95. Hobby House Press, Inc., 900 Frederick St., Cumberland, MD 21502. Paper doll postcards included in this book, but more importantly understanding paper dolls helps with an understanding of the paper toy postcards.

Neudin. *Postcard Catalogue*. (in French), Annual. 500-600p. ;ill. black & white and color, ISBN 2-90-2972-22-4: Neudin, 35 rue G., St. Hilaire, Paris, France 75005. If you collect European views or art cards this is a must. One of the best postcard catalogues available. Things get lost being shipped. Try to find a dealer going to Europe to bring it back for you. Buy back issues, they are full of information. They do one artist or topic in depth

BIBLIOGRAPHY

each year. The 1991 catalogue was on illustrators. Great books.

Nicholson, Susan Brown. *Mickey Mouse Memorabilia*; *The Vintage Years 1928-1938*. 1986. 180p. ;ill. 17 of postcards, 300 others, ISBN 0-8109-1439-5: $30.00. Harry N. Abrams, New York, NY. Out of print.

Nicholson, Susan Brown. *Teddy Bears on Paper*. 1985. 127p. ;ill. 500 black & white and color, ISBN 0-917205-03-0: $50.00. Taylor Publishing Company, Dallas, Texas. Out of print. Occasionally available from the author, Nicholson, P.O. Box 595, Lisle, IL 60532. This book was very successful and a delight for Teddy Bear collectors.

Nudelman, Edward D. *Jessie Wilcox Smith: American Illustrator*. 1990. 144p. ;ill. 200 color, ISBN 0-88289-786-1: $39.95. Pelican Publishing Co., 1101 Monroe Street, Gretna, LA 70053. A biography worth reading. Delightful illustration.

Olson, Richard. *The R. F. Outcault Collection*. 22p. ;ill. none, Richard Olson, 103 Doubloon Drive, Slidell, LA 70461.

Ouellette, William. *Fantasy Postcards*. 1975. 87p. ;ill. 252 black & white and color, ISBN 0-385-11230-0 (paperback) 0-385-11175-4 (hardcover): Doubleday and Company, Inc., Garden City, New York, NY. Out of print. Enjoy this one at the library, Ouellette taught us all how to look at cards differently.

Ouellette & Jones. *Erotic Postcards*. 1977. 127p. ;ill. 250 black & white and color, ISBN 0-525-70054-4: Excalibur Books, 201 Park Ave. S., New York, NY 10003. A super look at turn of the century humor and romance.

Papell & Lowe. *Detroit Publishing Company Collectors' Guide*. 1975. 288p. ;ill. none, ISBN 0-913782-07-6: Deltiologists of America, P.O. Box 8, Norwood, PA 19074.

Parkin, Michael. *Louis Wain's Cats*. 1983. 79p. ;ill. 62, 32 in color, ISBN 0-500-01319-5: Thames and Hudson, England. Biography and great illustrations.

Reade, Brian. *Louis Wain*. 1972. 27p. ;ill. 14 color. Victoria & Albert Museum, England. Biography and delightful illustrations.

Reed, Walter & Roger. *The Illustrator in America 1880-1980*. 1984. 355p. ;ill. 700 black & white and color, ISBN 0-94260403-2: The Society of Illustrators, New York, NY.

Rickards, Maurice. *Collecting Printed Ephemera*. 1988. 224p. ;ill. 600 black & white and color, ISBN 0-89659-893-4: $35.00. Abbeville Press, Inc., 488 Madison Avenue, New York, NY 10022. Great book on general ephemera.

Rosenblum, Robert. (Introduction) Essays by Hellen Harrison, Ileen Sheppard et al. *Remembering The Future: The New York World's Fair From 1939 to 1964*. 1989. 208p. ;ill. 225 black & white and color, ISBN 0-8478-1122-0: Rizzoli, New York, NY. The history and architecture is fully explored by numerous essays.

Rubin & Williams. *Larger Than Life; The American Tall-Tale Postcard, 1905-1915*. 1990. 132p. ;ill. 250 black & white, ISBN 1-55850-014-5: Abbyeville Press, Inc., 488 Madison Avenue, New York, NY 10022. A delightful book about exaggerations.

Ruggles, Rowena Godding. *The One Rose; Mother of the Immortal Kewpies*. 1964, 1972. 96p. ;ill. 200 black & white. Ruggles, Albany, CA 94706. Out of print. A must have book for the Kewpie collector. Sells for $85-150 depending on edition.

Ryan, Dorothy. *Picture Postcards in the United States 1893-1918*. 1982. 280p. ;ill. 200 black & white and color, ISBN 0-517-524007 (hardcover), 0-517-545888 (paperback): Clarkson N. Potter, Inc., New York, NY. Out of print. If you are a serious collector, find this book. Libraries have it in hardbound under Miller, first edition. Occasionally available from

BIBLIOGRAPHY

Greater Chicago Productions, P.O. Box 595, Lisle, IL. 60532.

Ryan, Dorothy. *Philip Boileau: Painter of Fair Women, Postcard artist and Illustrator*. 1981. 77p. ;ill. 20 black & white and color, ISBN 910664-47-1: Gotham Book Mart, 41 West 47th St., New York, NY 10036. A good checklist and biography of artist.

Saleh, Nouhad A. *Guide to Artists' Signatures & Monograms on Postcards*. 1993. 395p. ;ill. 450 black & white, ISBN 0-9636078-0-4: $70.00. Minerva Press, Inc., P.O. Box 969, Boca Raton, FL 33429.

Salt, Mark H. *Candidates and the Issues; An Official history of the Campaign of 1908*. 1908. 430p. ;ill. 40 black & white. Charles B. Ayer. Out of print. Political collectors look for this in Antique shops, it gives actual speeches and platforms. Learn from the candidates mouth what they stood for and dreamed.

Schau, Michael. *All-American Girl: The Art of Coles Phillips*. 1975. 176p. ;ills. 250 black & white and color, ISBN 0-8230-0173-3: Watson-Guptil, New York, NY. Out of print.

Schnessel, S. Michael. *Jessie Wilcox Smith*. 224p. ;ill. 200 black & white and color, ISBN 0-690-01493-7: Thomas Y. Crowell, New York, NY. Out of print. A carefully done biography of JWS.

Schnessel, S. Michael. *Icart*. 1976. 178p. ;ill. 300 black & white and color, ISBN 0-517-52498-8: Clarkson N. Potter, New York, NY. A well researched biography of Icart.

Silvester & Mobbs. *A Catland Companion*. 1991. 96p. ;ill. 250 color, $20.00. Summit Books, New York, NY. Classic cats by Wain and others dot every page of this book with whimsical copy. A fun book.

Silvester & Mobbs. *The Cat Fancier; A Guide to Catland Postcards*. 1982. 128p. ;ill. 300 black & white and color, ISBN 0-582-503124: Longman, London, England. A nice catalog of cat postcards, lists title, publishers and artists when known. A nice reference.

Smith, Darrell A. *Black Americana; A Personal Collection*. 1988. 322p. ;ill. 900 in color, $36.95. Black Relics, Inc., P.O. Box 24954, Tempe, AZ 85282. About 300 of the color illustrations are of postcards. An informative book.

Smith, Demaris C. *Preserving Your Paper Collectibles*. 1989. 184p. ;ill. 60 black & white and color, ISBN 1-55870-125-7: $14.95. Betterway Publications, Inc., Whitehall, VA. This is a comprehensive guide to protecting paper collectibles. Well worth reading.

Spencer, Charles. *Leon Bakst*. 1973. 248p. ;ill. 400 black & white and color, ISBN 0-8478-0203-5: Rizzoli, New York, NY. A fascinating biography of Bakst. Some cards illustrated.

Staff, Frank. *The Picture Postcard and its Origins*. 1966. 96p. ;ill. 138, ISBN 0-7188-2410-5: Frederick A. Praeger, New York, NY. Out of print. For the best history of cards, find this book. Occasionally available from Greater Chicago Productions, P.O. Box 595, Lisle, IL 60532.

Staff, Frank. *Picture Postcards and Travel*. 1979. 96p. ;ill. 400 black & white and color, ISBN 0-7188-2410-5: Lutterworth Press, London, England. Out of print. A beautiful book featuring many wonderful Gruss Aus postcards from before the turn of the century.

Staff, Frank. *The Valentine and Its Origin*. 1969. 143p. ;ill. 250 black & white and color. Frederick A. Praeger, New York, NY. Out of print. A superb book to track down. The history of the early greeting cards teach us how the paper collectibles started. Any book written by Frank Staff is worth buying regardless of age. Occasionally available from Greater Chicago Productions, P.O. Box 595, Lisle, IL. 60532.

Sturani, Enrico. *Nuove Cartoline, Cartoline postali di ieri e di oggi in un'ottica d'avanguardia*.

(in Italian), 1981. 80p. ;ill. 400 black & white and color. Savelli Editori, Rome, Italy. Great documentary on modern cards as well as early cards. Leans towards the avant-garde.

Tucker, Kerry. *Greetings from New York; A Visit to Manhattan in Postcards.* 1981. 112p. ;ill. 100 black & white and color, ISBN 0-933328-04-4: Delilah Books, New York, NY. A history of the tourist attractions of New York through vintage postcards. A refreshing approach to a tourist guide.

Venman, Smith, Mead, & Konec. *The Postcard Catalogue 1993.* Annual. 158p. ;ill. 300 black & white and color, $20.00. IPM Publications, 6 Barons Walk, Lewis, Sussex BN7 1EX, England. The English dealers follow this price guide to the letter. Be aware of trends on the European market.

Vessup, Aaron. *Symbolic Communication: Understanding Racial Stereotypes that Persist.* 1983. 81p. ;ill. 100 black & white. Brethren Press, Elgin, IL. A resulting project from a Faculty Development Grant, Dept. of Non-Traditional Education, Elgin Community College. While many Afro-American paper and other collectibles are illustrated, the text is very limited in understanding the media or the message.

Wallis, Michael. *Route 66, The Mother Road.* 1990. 242p. ;ill. 300 black & white and color, ISBN 0-312-04049-0: St. Martin's Press, New York, NY. Documentation of the road from Chicago to California. Great for collectors of Route 66 postcards.

Ward, Robert. *Investment Guide to North American Real Photo Postcards.* 1992. 246p. ;ill. 325 black & white, $33.95. Antique Paper Guild, P.O. Box 5742, Bellevue, WA 98006.

Warr & Lawson. *The Postcards of Lance Thackery.* 1979. 56p. ;ill. 60 black & white. Postcards for Pleasure, Middlesex, England. A checklist of the artists work and small biography.

Warr & Lawson. *The Postcards of Tom Browne.* 1978. 64p. ;ill. 250 black & white. Postcards for Pleasure, London, England. A checklist of the artists work and a small biography.

Weill, Alain. *Art Nouveau Postcards.* 1977. 80p. ;ill. 128 color, ISBN 0-89545-014-3: Image Graphiques, Inc., 37 Riverside Drive, New York, NY 10023. Beautifully illustrated book with small biography of each artist.

Weill, Alain. *Alphonse Mucha: toutes les Cartes postales.* (All the Postcards) (in French, English & German) 1983. 136p. ;ill. 300 color, ISBN 91-970091-2-1: Hjert & Hjert, Sweden. The quality of the European books always seem superior. This is no exception, nearly all postcards in color and nearly all pictured. A great book for any postcard collector, whether or not you collect Mucha.

Williams, Anne D. *Jigsaw Puzzles; An Illustrated History and Price Guide.* 1990. 362p. ;ill. 800 black & white and color, $24.95. Wallace Homestead, Des Moines, IA. This book includes many postcard puzzles but more importantly gives a very detailed history of the puzzle. Great reading.

Wood, Jane. *The Collector's Guide to Post Cards.* 1984. 175p. ;ill. 3,000 black & white and color. No text, out date prices.

Wykes, Alan. *Saucy Seaside Postcards.* 1977. 131p. ;ill. 140 black & white and color, ISBN 904041-66-2: Jupiter Books Ltd., London, England. Out of print. History of seaside as well as erotic seaside postcards.

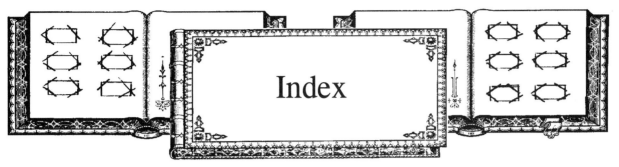

Index

Italicised entries are titles of books, magazines, newspapers, etc. Numbers in italic refer to pages with illustrations of the entry subject.

INDEX

INDEX

INDEX

INDEX

INDEX

INDEX

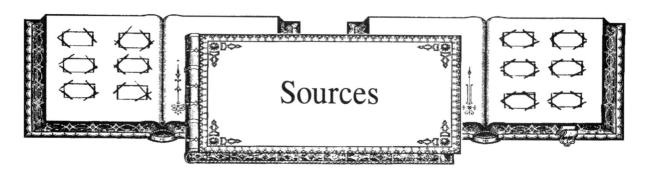

Sources

This section will prove useful in identifying where antique postcards can be purchased or sold. The trade paper, Barr's Postcard News, has weekly auction ads with the cards illustrated. It is a great place to run want ads and has an extensive show calendar section. I have a regular Sets and Series column in this publication illustrating cards. The Postcard Collector is a monthly magazine with informative articles and classified ads. I have a regular column, Pursuing the Marvelous, in this publication, which gives detailed information about sets, plus illustrations.

The dealers listed in this section were chosen for their integrity, quality of merchandise, and responsiveness to customers. Most handle a variety of cards. Read the ads carefully. Some do not handle view cards or do mail order. When writing advertisers, enclose a self addressed stamped envelope and mention you saw their ad in this book.

Greater Chicago Productions has three Antique Ephemera shows each year, specializing in postcards. Stop and visit with us the next time you're in town.

Greater Chicago Postcard Show

3 Times a Year Write for Show Dates or Dealer Inquiries

Over 100 Tables with Quality Dealers from Twenty States
Susan Brown Nicholson
Box 595, Lisle, IL 60532

256

An International Firm dealing in England and the USA

Largest stock of Foreign cards in the USA

Wide selection of Artist Signed, Poster Art, Propangada, Hold to Lights, Transportation, and Holidays: Halloween, Santas, & Valentines

We buy all Foreign and Domestic postcards

Half a million postcards in our shop, plus Posters, Books, Calendars, Advertising, Toys, and Antiques

CHRIS RUSSELL
and
THE HALLOWEEN QUEEN

P.O. Box 499
4 Lawrance Street at Route 10
Winchester, NH 03470
603-239-8875

In Business since 1958 -- You can rely on us to treat you fairly

Home of the **TRICK OR TREAT TRADER**, a publication dedicated to the preservation and history of an American Holiday, Halloween and its artifacts.

Publishers of the Whitney Halloween Postcard Checklist.

SOURCES

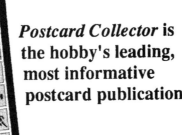
263

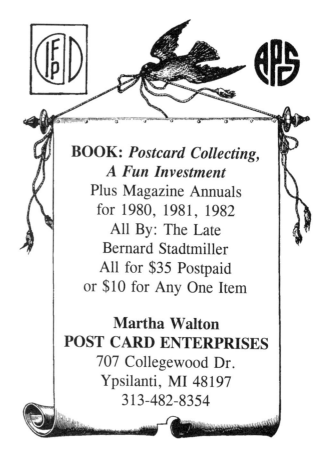

Nurses Wanted!

I collect postcards depicting nurses. I am particularly interested in quality material, U.S. and foreign, including signed artist, exceptional real photo, advertising, documentary, pioneer... anything unusual, striking, or significant.

I can also use postcards of related topics (which need not picture a nurse) such as Red Cross and other health organizations, anti-TB and other disease crusades, hygiene conventions, poster style advertisements for medicines, hospital fund raising, etc.

Please send approvals or photocopies. I reimburse for all expenses and make returns within 48 hours of receipt. Correspondence is welcome and will be answered promptly.

Michael Zwerdling, R.N.
Post Office Box 240
Boston, MA 02130

SOURCES

271

SOURCES

Collector
Wants To Buy
Real Photo
Exaggeration Postcards
Co-Author of

LARGER
THAN LIFE

Autographed Copies Available
For $27.95 Postpaid
E. Morgan Williams
P.O. Box 2607
Washington, DC 20013
Phone/Fax: 703-425-5866

Magnets
From Your
Favorite
Postcard Or
Photograph
Or From Our
Many Catagories
Such As:
Advertising
Automobiles
Baseball
Blacks
Cats
Clapsaddles
Halloween
Santas

Actual Size

Reproduction is exact and in color.
Five magnets $10 ppd. or sample $2.50

Postcard Images
P.O. Box 6783, Portland ME 04101

AMERICAN
EXPOSITION POSTCARDS

1870-1920

WITH PRICE GUIDE

An Encyclopedia of Information

280 Pages
1100 Illustrations
Publisher Identification Guide

Glossary
Complete Index
Realistic Prices

PRICE $21.50 P.P.
THE POSTCARD LOVERS
Frederic and Mary Megson
Box 482, Martinsville, NJ 08836

Authors of Sets and Series of American Advertising Postcards, 1890-1920.

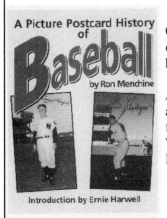

NOTES